W9-BIJ-111
KNOW THEIR JOB
ORT
ACK
PRACTICE
DISCIPLINE
GATE
ORK
ASSESS
PERFORMANCE
SET TARGETS

"Perhaps there is nothing more important to the success of an organization than a well-functioning Board. Whether a local government or a non-profit, achievement is dependent on the synergy between the Board and the staff. Mike, Carol and Catherine have described in a creative and entertaining way the behaviors of effective governance that will work for every Board."

Bob O'Neill,
Executive Director International City/County Management Association and Academy Fellow, National Academy of Public Administration

"Wow—what a great read! You nailed it!! I'm amazed at the clever story line doing such a great job of weaving in so many key messages. Big time kudos."

Bill Charney,
CEO & Principal Consultant, Charney Associates

"Great organizations are all about great governance. These 8 Indisputable Behaviors will help a weak board become strong and a good board become great."

Thomas M. Skiba, *Chief Executive Officer, Community Associations Institute*

"*The OnTarget Board Member* is a very light, pleasant and easy read. I did not put it down once I started it and was so engrossed I did not realize how the time went by. Having been involved with policy governance for quite a few years now, this story encapsulated the essence of good governance in a very practical and easy to understand way."

Dr. S. Eshwar Kumar MBBS, FRCR,
Chair Canadian Cancer Society, New Brunswick Division

"The OnTarget Board Member creates a believable world where board behaviors can make a true difference…a treat to read!"

Carol Anne Duffy, *CEO, Worker Compensation Board of Prince Edward Island*

"After 26 years of sitting through countless city council and other board meetings, I believe *The OnTarget Board Member* clearly hits the mark on effective behaviors that can improve board member performance and increase organizational productivity. The message creeps up on you and suddenly you find yourself thinking about your own experiences and how they can be improved with OnTarget behaviors."

Jim Hunt, *2006 American City and County Magazine Municipal Official of the Year, Past President on the National League of Cities, and City Council member, Clarksburg, West Virginia*

"The OnTarget Board Member is very informative – and especially well-written. It holds valuable information for setting roles and direction for any board."

Carolyn Corbin, *Founder and President, The Center for the 21st Century*

"Great learning comes from great story telling, and this is governance story telling at its best. Read the book, savor the story, absorb the behaviors, and get yourself and your board OnTarget!"

Stuart Emslie, CEO, *UK Policy Governance® Association*

"What a pleasure to read a story about the use of my principles by responsible, capable boards. The authors have brought the Policy Governance® experience to life."

Dr. John Carver, *creator of the Policy Governance model, author and consultant*

"This is a highly readable and very enjoyable tale which clearly outlines some important principles of the Carver Policy Governance® model. A great learning tool!"

Miriam Carver, *author and Policy Governance consultant*

The OnTarget Board Member

The OnTarget Board Member

8 INDISPUTABLE BEHAVIORS

Michael A. Conduff, Carol M. Gabanna, Catherine M. Raso

Published by Elim Group Publishing.

Photograph of conference table on front cover is used courtesy of Herman Miller Canada Inc.

ISBN: 978-0-9794875-9-0

Contents

Authors' Personal Note....9
Acknowledgements....11
Foreword....13
Chapter 1: Allied Headquarters....19
Chapter 2: The Breakfast....23
Chapter 3: The Questions....27
Chapter 4: The Seminar....31
Chapter 5: Allied Headquarters....37
Chapter 6: Joe's Office....43
Chapter 7: The Boardroom....55
Chapter 8: The Cafeteria....59
Chapter 9: The Food Bank Board Meeting....65
Chapter 10: The Parking Garage....79
Chapter 11: Starbucks....87
Chapter 12: The Newsroom....91
Chapter 13: The Story....95
Epilogue: Six Months Later....103
Sneak Peek....104
Appendices....116
Authors' Biographies....135
Bibliography....141

Authors' Personal Note

EACH OF US CAME to Policy Governance® from different paths. Mike was the city manager of a Texas community. Once his council adopted the model, they asked him to become proficient in it. Carol was the CEO of a hospital association in Charlottetown, Prince Edward Island, and as a passionate reader had devoured *Boards That Make a Difference*, when it was newly published. Catherine was the CEO of a nonprofit organization in Hamilton, Ontario. She and her board chair realized that Policy Governance would resolve their governance issues.

Fortunately, these paths intersected, and the three of us met at the inaugural Policy Governance Academy in Atlanta in 1995. Strangers from different countries when class began, our passion for good governance fueled an immediate friendship that has blossomed over the ensuing years.

We followed the Academy with facilitating a series of international symposia, the first of which was "PEI in July" held in Carol's community in 1996. Following that inaugural gathering, for many years the best and brightest practitioners from around the globe have gathered annually to advance the body of knowledge associated with this incredible and powerful model.

Along the way, we were three of the coauthors of the *Policy Governance Fieldbook* and have contributed articles to *Board Leadership* and other scholarly journals. Each of us worked with many boards to expand our own knowledge and to assist others. We have also served on boards—traditional boards as well as Policy Governance boards. All in all, it has been a great journey.

The OnTarget Board Member is our attempt to bring the behaviors of good governance to the incredible number of fabulous people who actually serve on boards. We offer governance training sessions all over the world, so please visit our websites to find dates and locations.

It is our pleasure to welcome you to the world of the OnTarget Board Member!

Enjoy!

Acknowledgements

AS AUTHORS WE ARE especially grateful to the cadre of individuals who assisted us with this effort. Weaving a fable around solid principles requires much effort, and we were quite blessed with the support we received.

We want to thank the participants in the Eighth Annual International Policy Governance Symposium in Toronto where this journey began for their enthusiastic participation and generous contribution of thought surrounding best practice board behavior.

Many of our colleagues in the governance arena read the manuscript at various stages and offered suggestions, criticisms and comments. Our sincere thanks to Larry Spears, Randy Quinn, Phil Graybeal, Kandy and Peter Rose, Matthew Park, Bob O'Neill, Jim Hunt, Chris Bart, Eshwar Kumar, Stuart Emslie, Tom Skiba, Carol Anne Duffy and John and Miriam Carver.

Our administrative support was a team effort and Kathy Conduff, David Chanasyk and Nancy Cupido are owed a debt of gratitude.

Thanks to Jd Howell for his creativity and patience in creating our logo and cover design for all three editions.

The folks at RJ Communications were professional, supportive and patient. Particular thanks goes to Jonathan Gullery for his able assistance with the manuscript and polishing the many pieces of the book.

Finally we especially want to thank our families. Jobs and lives go on while writing takes place, so much of this work took time away from them. We love you guys!

Mike, Carol and Catherine

Foreword to The OnTarget Board Member

LARRY C. SPEARS, PRESIDENT EMERITUS
AND GREENLEAF SENIOR FELLOW
THE GREENLEAF CENTER FOR SERVANT LEADERSHIP

THIS VERY VALUABLE BOOK that you hold begins with the fundamental principle that boards must first be servants of their owners. *The OnTarget Board Member* is a wonderful example of how boards can practically approach this vital, yet often neglected, work.

Mike, Carol, and Catherine use their unique understanding of Carver's and Greenleaf's concepts to bring Joe Victor to life. Joe, while "OnTarget" as a board member, is first and foremost a servant-leader.

Robert K. Greenleaf (1904–1990) coined the term *servant-leadership* in his 1970 essay, "The Servant as Leader." Although he created the term, he did not invent servant-leadership. Indeed, servant-leadership has been with us for thousands of years. Servant-leadership is practiced today by people from all walks of life. Anyone can be a servant-leader. The Greenleaf Center has among its members people of many different faiths, philosophies, and secular beliefs. What they all have in common is their commitment to growing as servant-leaders.

Robert Greenleaf defined the servant-leader this way:

> The servant-leader is servant first. It begins with the natural feeling that one wants to serve, to serve first. Then conscious choice brings one to aspire to lead. ... The best test is: Do those served grow as persons? Do they, while being served, become healthier, wiser, freer, more autonomous, more likely themselves to become servants? And, what is the effect on the least privileged in society; will they benefit or, at least, not be further deprived?

"THE SERVANT AS LEADER" (1970/1973)

In 1970 Greenleaf wrote "The Servant as Leader," privately printed 200 copies, and sent them to people who he thought might be interested in it. In 1973 he did a major revision of it, and it is the 1973 version that some recognize by its distinctive orange cover. Mostly by word of mouth, over a half-million copies of "The Servant as Leader" essay have been produced and sold over the past four decades. For such a modest-looking publication, it has had a profound impact on several generations of leaders and trustees.

Many of today's best-known leadership authors have become powerful advocates for servant-leadership, and they are involved with the Greenleaf Center as contributing authors to our books and as speakers at our conferences on servant-leadership. Among them are John Carver, James Autry, Max DePree, Warren Bennis, Ken Blanchard, Stephen Covey, Parker Palmer, Peter Senge, Margaret Wheatley, and many others.

"THE INSTITUTION AS SERVANT" (1972)

In 1972 Bob Greenleaf wrote "The Institution as Servant" in order to share his ideas on how institutions as well as individuals could become more servant-led.

Servant-leadership starts with the individual, but it has tremendous organizational applications as well. Many businesses and nonprofit institutions today have embraced servant-leadership. Among the better known are The Toro Company, ServiceMaster, The Men's Wearhouse, Southwest Airlines, TDIndustries, The Vanguard Group, Synovus Financial, U.S. Cellular, and Starbucks. Most if not all of these companies have also made an annual appearance on *Fortune* magazine's "100 Best Places to Work" list published each January. There are many other businesses, colleges, hospitals, and other kind of institutions where servant-leadership education and training is taking place and being practiced.

"TRUSTEES AS SERVANTS" (1974)

In 1974 Greenleaf wrote "Trustees as Servants," the third essay in his Servant series. He had begun with "The Servant as Leader," addressing individuals; turned to institutions with "The Institution as Servant"; and then examined boards of trustees as the entity with the greatest power to guide institutions toward a more servant-led nature.

"Trustees as Servants" was written for those who were dissatisfied with their present roles and who might venture to create a new role for themselves with a vision of greatness to guide them.

George Washington was noted for signing his letters, "Your most humble and obedient servant." "Trustees as Servants" is an argument in support of trustees choosing to be servant-leaders.

Some characteristics of servant-leaders and of trustees as servant-leaders are listening, empathy, healing, awareness, persuasion, conceptualization, foresight, stewardship, commitment to the growth of people, and building community.

GREENLEAF ON TRUSTEESHIP

In his essay "Trustees as Servants," Robert Greenleaf offers many important insights on the role of boards. Chief among them are the following:

- The role of the trustee board is to stand outside of the active work of the organization. It provides institutional vision.
- Trusteeship is the holding of a charter of public trust for an institution.
- The major trustee functions are:
    1. To set the goals, to define the obligation and the general concept of the institution, and to approve plans for reaching goals.
    2. To appoint the top administrative officers, to design the top administrative structure, to design and assign the duties of individuals in that group, and to act so as to motivate administrators and professionals.
    3. To assess, at appropriate times, the performance of the institution.
    4. To take appropriate action based on the above assessment.

SERVANT-LEADERSHIP AND POLICY GOVERNANCE IN TANDEM

In 1998 John Carver addressed the Greenleaf Center's International Conference on the theme of "The Unique Double Servant-Leadership Role of the Board Chairperson," and he said the following:

> Allow me to position Policy Governance with respect to Greenleaf's work. Peter Senge has observed that "recent books on leadership have been about what leaders do and how they operate." "By contrast, Greenleaf," Senge says, "invites people to consider a domain of leadership grounded in a state of being, not doing." The choice of servant-leadership, he explains, is "not something you do, but an expression of your being." Policy Governance is an operational definition (in its scientific meaning) of leadership in a specific setting—that of the governing body. In some ways, the difference Senge points out is like that between philosophy and strategy, or between basic research and technology. If the judgment of history is kind, the Policy Governance model may merit being seen as a technology of servant-leadership. At any rate, it is a carefully crafted prescription for how boards can operate—boards that are committed to being servant-leaders.

I believe that this is right On Target: servant-leadership is a philosophy of being; the Policy Governance Model is a great technology of servant-leadership.

Trustees who have a servant's heart can benefit through the understanding and practice of the Policy Governance Model. Likewise, practitioners of the Policy Governance Model may attain the truest expression of it by seeking to live as servant-leaders.

The OnTarget Board Member: 8 Indisputable Behaviors is aligned with the principles of Policy Governance and has provided the means for trustees to live out Greenleaf's challenge to boards to act as both servant and leader.

I believe the time has come to increasingly raise awareness and practices of both servant-leadership and Policy Governance in tandem with one another, rather than as separate ideas. In so doing, we may yet succeed in transforming the hearts and minds of individuals, institutions, and society.

Chapter 1

Allied Headquarters

JOE VICTOR LOOKED UP and smiled as Natalie Benson, his long-time chief of staff, walked into his carefully appointed Allied Technologies office, which overlooked the Chamton skyline, for their ritual kick-off-the-week strategy appointment. Smartly dressed as always, she had a half-dozen file folders, her iPad, her ever-present smartphone, and a list of messages to be returned.

"Hi, Joe," she said cheerfully. "How was your weekend?"

"It was fabulous," Joe replied. "Kids, a pool, a barbecue grill, and lots of sunshine: what more could you ask for? How was yours?"

"Excellent as well." And then, ever efficient, she added, "Shall we get started?"

Joe grinned, remembering their first encounter a dozen years earlier...

As a still young and already successful senior-level executive, he was a rising star at Allied and in the community, and he was a member of a half-dozen civic and philanthropic boards of directors. Although he felt good about where he was and what he had accomplished, at times it seemed his life was consumed by meetings, meetings, and more meetings. Many of these were for his volunteer boards, and they often were held at night and even on the weekends. Even though he really believed in the mission of these organizations, their board meetings left him feeling drained and frustrated. In his view, the meetings lasted much longer than they needed to and accomplished little. In fact, it seemed that most involved nothing more than listening to endless reports from staff and committees and approving actions that others had already taken or at least had decided to take.

After one particularly frustrating Saturday morning session, he had fumed all the way home and told his wife Patricia, “I feel like a rubber stamp for the executive director of the food bank! They spoon-feed me information and reports that I could easily read in advance and then expect me to vote on the spot. I’m tired of taking time from you and the kids for this. I really think they only want me for my donation checks and because of my position at Allied. I’m so busy, I just meet myself coming and going, and then when I get there, I don’t feel like I am contributing a bit. I’ve had it!”

Patricia had patted his arm understandingly and said, “I don’t like having you gone either. It’s just that the food bank and the other organizations do so much good in the community, and you have so much to offer them. You are the best, you know,” she teased.

Moving around to give him a hug, she said, “Before you just quit serving, I’d like you to meet my friend Natalie. She just moved back to Chamton. She is super organized and has been a CEO of a similar sort of nonprofit. Besides, she’s been telling me about some people she knows who work extensively with boards. Perhaps she can help you on a couple of fronts.”

True to her word, Patricia arranged for the three of them to get together. Natalie, who was as impressive then as she is now, listened to his concerns (Patricia later called it whining) and said, "Joe, don't give up just yet. Boards can make a difference in the world; you just need to know how to get yourself and those boards OnTarget!"

And that had been the beginning. Years later ...

Chapter 2

The Breakfast

AS NATALIE SAT DOWN at the round conference table, Joe took out his own smartphone and scooted his chair over. He was curious about the messages to be returned, because Natalie normally handled those or had Jan, his administrative assistant, pass them to him. He saw that the first one was from a young reporter Joe had only recently met at a Chamber of Commerce breakfast.

Natalie said, "This one is a bit unusual. This young man would like to have an interview with you. He is very persistent. I tried to run interference for you, but he asked if I would speak to you directly about him."

"Oh, I remember him," Joe replied. "If he's interested in our success here at Allied Tech, or how I became CEO, just send him to the public information office. They can give him what he needs."

"Actually," Natalie said, "he wants to talk personally with you. He is doing a story on how to be an effective board member. He told me on the phone that everyone in Chamton that he talks to says you are the best at that. He says they call you the OnTarget Board Member."

"Well, I have you to thank for that," Joe said.

After a brief pause, he said, "I'll tell you what. Why don't you see if he can join me for an hour for breakfast at the Galleria in the morning, and I will see if he has a teachable spirit."

Natalie nodded and wrote a quick note to herself on her smartphone.

"Now," said Joe, "what's next?"

The Next Morning

Arriving a few minutes early, as was his custom, Joe was pleased to observe that the young reporter already had a table and had left him the seat in the corner so that he could see others as they came into the restaurant.

"Mr. Victor," the reporter said, "my name is Ivan, Ivan John—I work for the *Sunday News*. We met at a Chamber event."

"Yes, Ivan, I remember you," Joe said with a smile. "What can I do for you?"

"Well, first of all, thanks so much for granting me this interview. As I am sure Mrs. Benson told you, I have been assigned to do a feature on the people behind the scenes of the nonprofits in town. Everyone I talk to refers me to you. In fact, they ask me if I have talked to the OnTarget Board Member yet. Why do they call you that?"

"Well, Ivan, first, please call me Joe. 'Mr. Victor' makes me feel way too old!"

Ivan nodded, and then Joe continued, "Mr. OnTarget is a nickname I acquired because of some people I met several years ago. They helped me see the value that boards and board members can provide to the world, and more importantly they taught me the behaviors I needed to know to be truly effective as a board member. These people believe that if board members know that there are recognizable behaviors that they should engage in or certain things that they should do, they will have a clearer understanding of their roles. Then they can attract and keep great board members, maintain discipline at the board table, and ultimately have more effective organizations."

Joe continued, "At first, I was a little skeptical, so each time I used one of their techniques, I would attribute it to them, just in case it flopped. That way, I wouldn't get tagged with it—plausible deniability and all of that." Joe grinned. "Of course, their concepts really worked, and so over time I just became known as the OnTarget Board Member—at first as in, 'Oh no, not another OnTarget comment!' and later as, 'Wow, what would an OnTarget Board Member do in this situation?'"

"You say you met the OnTarget Team a dozen years ago," Ivan said. "How did that occur?"

Joe grinned again, remembering his first meeting with Natalie and her consulting friends.

"Well," he said, "it's a good story. Let's order breakfast, and I'll share it with you."

Chapter 3

The Questions

AFTER THE WAITRESS HAD left, Joe looked at Ivan and said, "You have talked to Natalie Benson on the phone."

Ivan nodded and gestured good-naturedly. "Three or four times now. She guards you pretty well."

Joe acknowledged the comment with a nod and said, "Well, a dozen years ago, when I was one of the vice presidents at Allied, my lovely wife, Patricia, introduced me to her. It turns out Patricia and Natalie were friends from college. After graduation, Natalie went into the health care field, where she enjoyed much success and even became a young CEO of a nonprofit hospital support group. In that role, she worked closely with a board of directors made up of community volunteers, doctors, and hospital administrators."

Although he wondered where this story was headed, Ivan began taking notes. He also used his active listening skills to stay focused, knowing that Joe was a sought-after interview. After all, he had needed to be persistent with Mrs. Benson just to schedule this breakfast. Because most of his deadlines were late at night, he rarely saw this time of day.

Joe continued, "After a few years of constantly struggling with continuing budget challenges, huge personal time commitments, and the frustrations of working with a too-small staff, Natalie decided she wanted a change of venue and came back to Chamton. She intended to do some consulting and some life renewal."

"And that is where you met her," Ivan filled in.

"Correct," agreed Joe, pleased that Ivan was paying attention; he mentally acknowledged that indeed a teachable spirit seemed to be present. "I had about reached the breaking point with my own board volunteer positions, and Patricia thought Natalie could help me."

"Did she?" asked Ivan.

"I'll say," Joe said, nodding. "She knew the OnTarget Team."

Ivan brightened; this *was* turning into a good story.

"So you owe your success to your chief of staff?" he quizzed.

"Don't we all?" Joe responded with a smile.

"Level Five Leadership," Ivan quoted from Jim Collins's book *Good to Great*. "Give credit away."

"Exactly!" said Joe, leaning forward as he warmed to his story. "Patricia and Natalie and I had lunch one day. Natalie knew of my dissatisfaction with board service and so she asked me several questions about my experience such as, 'What is the purpose of the boards that you serve on? What is their real contribution to the organization? What is your role on these boards? What is expected of boards? What is expected of individual board members? What do you worry about as a board member? Do those boards know whether their organization is fulfilling its purpose?'

"At the time, I did not have good answers to her questions," Joe said. "In fact, I really had not thought of board service as anything other than raising money and just generally helping out. Finally she asked me a question I could answer."

Ivan leaned forward with his pen poised.

Joe looked at him and grinned. "She asked how often we met."

"Oh," said Ivan, looking a bit disappointed.

Joe continued, "I told her that most of the boards met at least once a month and that the Executive Committees met about twice that often."

"Why was that such an important question?" asked Ivan, still trying to stay focused despite the lack of sleep.

"Well, she followed it up with another one I could answer. She asked how often the Allied board met. 'Once a quarter', I responded.'

"'And, budget-wise, how do they compare?' she asked. 'Oh, they don't really,' I told her. 'Allied is over a billion a year, and most of the nonprofits are barely 1 or 2 or 3 percent of that.'

"'Why is it that at Allied', Natalie asked, 'which is in the business of making money for its shareholders and does a billion a year in business, the board chooses to meet once a quarter, and at the food bank, with a budget of one million, the board chooses to meet every month?'

"'My point is that most boards don't think about the frequency—or quality—of their meetings because they just do what's always been done. The issue is really the content and quality of the meetings, and whether the board is doing what is should be doing when it meets. Only then can the board determine how often, and how long, it needs to meet,' Natalie said.

"It began to dawn on me that if *I* was frustrated with lots of unproductive meeting time, perhaps others were too. After all, they were giving up their evenings and Saturdays as well. More importantly, I realized the reason the meetings felt unproductive was that we were not dealing with the important issues Natalie had raised.

"Then she zinged me again," Joe continued. "She asked what percentage of time the CEO of Allied spent with the board and asked me to compare that to the amount of time the CEO of, say a food bank, spends with hers.

"'The CEO of Allied spends significantly less time with his board than food bank CEO spends with hers, I replied confidently realizing there was another lesson coming.'

"'They are both governing boards, aren't they?' Natalie said. 'Then the two experiences shouldn't be so vastly different. Neither is necessarily right or wrong, but I wonder if either board has been clear about which decisions it's comfortable delegating and which strategic decisions are the board's to make.'

"'Okay, your points are made—boards need to be clear about their roles and their delegation' I said to Natalie. 'Give me some advice. What should I do next?'

"'Well, first,' Natalie said, 'I think you should go to this seminar my friends at OnTarget are doing in Toronto,' and then she handed me a brochure. 'You need to learn about the behaviors of high achieving boards.'

"'And second?' I asked."'Second,' she said, 'you should hire me to help you out at Allied. Patricia tells me you are in need of someone with my skills. I can certainly free up some of your time so you can continue to serve.'"

"Wow, that was bold!" interjected Ivan.

"Sure was," agreed Joe.

Chapter 4

The Seminar

"DID YOU GO TO the seminar?" asked Ivan.

"Yes, I did," assented Joe, nodding. "Best move I ever made! In fact, at Natalie's suggestion, I took Patricia, along. She loved Toronto. It is a beautiful city and full of friendly people and great restaurants. And I must say, the seminar was indeed a turning point for me, although I was surprised when I first walked into the seminar room."

"Why is that?" asked Ivan.

"Well, there were half a dozen round tables, and each one was covered with different kinds of balls, toy animals, colored cards, and fluorescent sticky notes. It looked like a circus! And besides, there was some kind of classical music playing. I considered myself to be a strong performer, sort of a stereotypical type A personality, and touchy-feely stuff just did not appeal to me."

"Wow," Ivan said. "That setup does sound odd."

Joe nodded and continued, "No sooner was I in the room than three of the nicest individuals you would ever want to meet came up to me and put me totally at ease. They were so genuine and caring, I knew I had to stay just to watch them work and see what they had to say.

"To begin the seminar, they introduced themselves and their passion for governance. Then they went on to point out the adult learning methodologies they used to get participants fully engaged in the learning."

"So that was the purpose of all the stuff—the adult learning part?" asked Ivan.

"Exactly," said Joe. "And then, after some introductions—well done, by the way—they fully caught my attention with their opening thought: that boards indisputably are powerful entities, concerned about what good the organization should be doing on behalf of its ownership in exchange for the resources that the community is willing to provide. In other words, the board is focused on the big picture."

"But I thought you said this was about nonprofit boards," objected Ivan. "Why were they talking about owners? Nonprofits don't have stockholders."

"Exactly my thought at the time," Joe replied. "They showed us that even nonprofits have owners—they referred to them as 'moral owners,' and knowing who those moral owners are is critical to a board being effective. In fact, they referred to the work of Robert K. Greenleaf, who, in 1970, coined the term *servant-leaders,* which is a philosophy of leadership based on the belief that to effectively lead, we must first understand our servant role. Boards serve these owners, listen to the owners, and of course are accountable to them as well. Then the board can truly lead the organization.

"And they taught us over the course of the weekend that there are 8 behaviors that these boards must indisputably demonstrate. Their work shows that if boards stay 'on target' with the behaviors, then board members' time and skills will be better used; that the board will have the information it needs to hold the CEO accountable and in turn be fully accountable to the owners. They called it the OnTarget Behaviors."

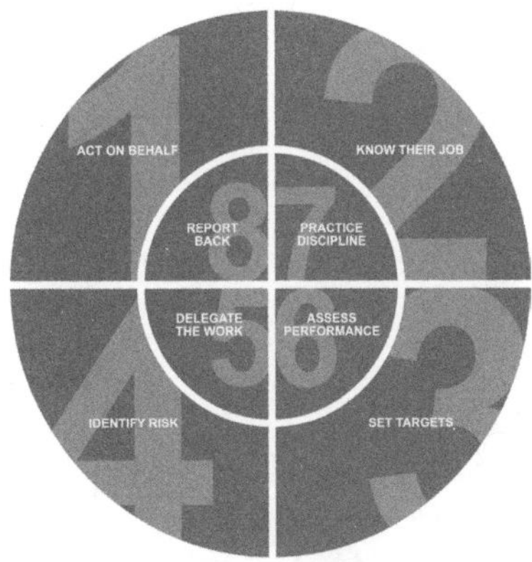

"I see," said Ivan, writing down *The OnTarget Behaviors* and underlining it and the number 8. "So the first thing that OnTarget Board Members must do is begin with understanding and clarifying to whom the board is morally accountable."

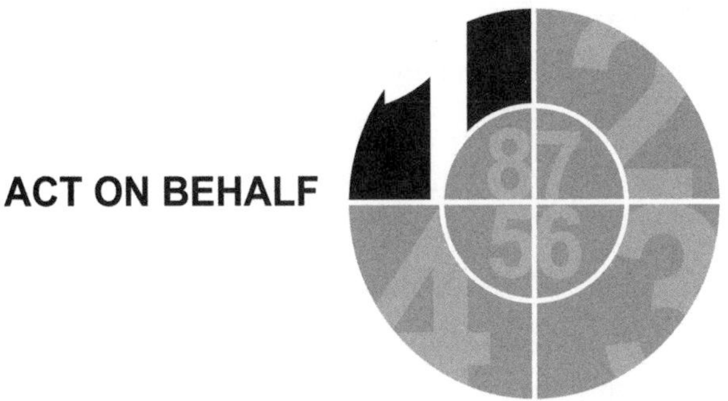

"Right again," said Joe, pausing to stand and shake the hand of a new arrival who had come by the table to greet Joe.

"Where were we?" he asked as he sat back down. "Oh yes, owners."

Joe went on, "On behalf of those owners, I, as a board member, have to decide with my colleagues what it is that the organization exists to achieve. The OnTarget Team called it 'the exchange with the world.' I would have called it 'organizational mission,' but they used the word *target*, meaning whatever the ultimate goal is.

"And so they asked us to think about who the customers of the organization are and how they would be better off because the organization exists."

"But nonprofits don't have customers; they have clients," said Ivan, shaking his head. "In fact, that is why nonprofits are always fund-raising and chasing grants; nobody pays for their service."

"True," Joe agreed. "Nonprofits lack a market test because clients usually don't pay the full cost of producing the service received. And so the OnTarget Team had us think about the difference between owners and customers. It was a great discussion about being either proactive or reactive. Owners arrive on the scene first so that customers' needs can be served."

Joe continued, “Once we know who our owners are and what they want us to accomplish, we can set clear targets for what the organization must achieve to improve people’s lives. Equally as important, we need to report back to them as to how well the organization did in achieving those targets.”

Joe and Ivan talked about owners and customers and targets for quite a while, then Joe’s smartphone began to vibrate. “Oh, has it been ninety minutes already? I’m afraid I must get on the road to my meeting with the chamber president. You know traffic!”

“But you were just getting to the good part!” exclaimed Ivan. “Is there another time we can get together this week? My deadline is Friday midnight.”

Looking at his smartphone, Joe said, “I’ll tell you what. Come by my office at Allied Thursday right after lunch, and we can finish then. And, by the way, Ivan, I’ve enjoyed getting to know you better. You are a talented young man.”

“Thanks, Mr. Victor—I mean Joe,” said Ivan. “See you Thursday.”

After Joe had left, Ivan reviewed his several pages of notes and, as was his habit, circled the points that seemed to be the most critical. He circled the following:

- 8 Indisputable Behaviors of OnTarget Boards
- They include the following:
    - o Acting on behalf of the owners
    - o Understanding the difference between customers and owners
    - o Being accountable to the owners
    - o Setting targets for the organization to achieve

Chapter 5

Allied Headquarters

ON THURSDAY, IVAN SHOWED up at Allied early. It was a big building, and he did not want to be late. From his research, he knew that Joe was unfailingly punctual, and he was determined not to get off on the wrong foot. Besides, he had been as impressed with Joe as people had told him he would be and didn't want to miss any opportunity to spend time with him.

As he entered the building, he was struck with the activity level. People were clearly engaged in their work, but everyone seemed very pleasant, even happy. This was quite a change from the newspaper office, where it seemed that everyone was generally grumpy, and editors were busy hollering at reporters about deadlines.

The atrium was warm, light, and inviting, and everywhere Ivan looked, he saw large, colorful pictures of Allied employees. Some were getting awards, and some were obviously posing in front of projects. On one wall was a banner that read AT ALLIED, OUR MOST VALUABLE ASSET IS OUR EMPLOYEES, and the wall was covered with pictures of adults with children of all ages.

Ivan noticed a young woman leave a small group of her colleagues and head in his direction. Like everything about

Allied she seemed very together. Smartly dressed she made eye contact with Ivan, and as she came closer she said, "Excuse me, may I help you with something?"

"Yes," said Ivan, still looking around. "But first, what are all of these pictures? I get the part about employees being an asset. Most companies say it, although few really mean it. What I don't understand is the pictures."

The woman smiled at Ivan. "Here at Allied we consider ourselves a team and a family. These pictures are our five- and ten-year employees with *their* families. Joe always says, 'You have to put your family first. If things aren't right at home, you can't be right at work.'"

"By 'Joe,' do you mean Mr. Victor?" asked Ivan.

"Yes," she said with a laugh. "But everyone here calls him Joe. He says Mr. Victor makes him sound too old."

"Wow," said Ivan, remembering that Joe had said that very thing to him at breakfast earlier in the week. "This is too good to be true."

"Oh, it's true all right. Joe is one of the reasons that Allied is regularly voted one of the best places in the greater Chamton area to work."

Half to himself, Ivan said, "I wouldn't mind working here myself."

At this, the young woman cleared her throat gently and said, "Now, how is it that I can help you?"

"Well, actually, I am here to see Mr. Vi … I mean Joe," Ivan replied. "Can you tell me how to get to his office?"

"Actually, I will be happy to take you there myself. Joe says we should amaze our customers, and one way to do that is to go and show, not point and tell. By the way, my name is Susan; let's walk this way."

"Thanks, Susan," Ivan said. "My name is Ivan." He was still amazed at the Allied atmosphere.

Riding the glass elevator with Susan, Ivan was surprised to see people clustered in small groups on every floor; some were in glass conference rooms, laughing with and nodding at their colleagues. He didn't think they were loafing, but he noted that the atmosphere at Allied was 180 degrees different from the newsroom's atmosphere.

"Is it always like this around here?" he asked his guide.

"Pretty much," Susan said with a nod. "Joe empowers all his teammates. He says that he doesn't really believe in rules and regulations. Because we are all adults, he prefers principles and values. It is the way the Board of Directors treats him, and that's the way he treats us."

"Say more about that Board of Directors thing," requested Ivan.

"Sure! First, we have customer service targets, and then our board has a list of things they do not want to occur on the way there. They visit this list about once a year and refine it if necessary."

"Allied is a big company," Ivan said. "It must be a long list."

"No, it's actually pretty short. The board says they basically want to make sure that nothing illegal, imprudent, or unethical goes on here. These are the board's values about how the organization is run. They are the risks that the board considers are unacceptable for us to take. Then it's up to us to further define that. In fact, if you would like, I can e-mail you a copy of our boundaries."

"Hey, that would be great," Ivan said. "What did you call them? Boundaries?" He took out his notebook.

"Yes, they are called staff boundaries," replied Susan.[1] "The board has a list for Joe, and then Joe and the vice presidents use that list to develop departmental boundaries. We call that 'Freedom through Limits' here at Allied. It is like raising your kids. You can never tell them all the things they can do, but you can easily tell them a few things they should never do because they are unacceptable."

"Well, here we are," said Susan as the elevator stopped at the top floor. "Joe's office is right here. Let me make sure you

[1] See Appendix 2

get introduced to Jan, Joe's assistant. In fact, she probably has those boundaries on her desk."

"Hi, Susan," said the woman rising from her desk and coming around to shake hands. "And you must be Ivan John. My name is Jan. I am Joe's assistant."

"Hello, Jan," Ivan said. "It is my pleasure to meet you. Susan here has been telling me quite a bit about the Allied culture. She's a great tour guide."

"Yes, Susan is on our superstar watch list. We have great things in store for her here at Allied."

Susan blushed and said, "Well, I better get back to my shop. It was nice to meet you, Ivan. Here is my card. If you need anything, please give me a call."

"Now, Jan … may I call you 'Jan'? Now, Jan, I noticed that you said 'Mr. Victor,' but everyone else seems to call him 'Joe,'" said Ivan, feeling his investigative journalism juices perk up.

"It's an old habit. My parents insisted on manners while I was growing up, and I really have to work at calling Mr. Victor 'Joe.' He has to remind me every now and then. May I offer you a beverage?"

"Why yes, water would be great. Say, Susan was telling me about some work the board has done called … let me see … oh yes, boundaries. She said you might have them."

"Actually, if you want to take a look on the wall over there, you can see our most current list."

"You keep your board's policies on the wall?" asked Ivan incredulously. "Aren't you afraid someone will steal Allied secrets?"

Jan laughed. "Joe says that the board wants people to know what they're supposed to be accomplishing. He calls it 'governance transparency.' Joe says that it is hard for people to hit the bull's-eye unless they know what the target is. That's what the board does. They give us a target, define boundaries, and then let us use our skill and talents to hit the target."

"Wow, can I quote you on that?" asked Ivan. "That is about the most concise statement I have ever heard about board work. No wonder this place is so successful!"

While Jan was out getting his water, Ivan wrote the following in his notebook:

- Boards set targets, delegate achievement to staff
- Boards also define boundaries—principles and values, limits on behavior
    - Like raising your kids—a few important "may nots"
- Freedom through Limits

Chapter 6

Joe's Office

WHEN JAN RETURNED WITH a water garnished with lemon in a crystal glass, she said, "Joe will meet with you in his office, and he's on his way up now. Let me go ahead and get you situated."

Ivan's eyes lit up as he walked into Joe's office. "So this is what it is like to be CEO of a Fortune 100 company! Nice digs."

Joe's office looked out over the impressive Chamton skyline. On his walls were pictures of what appeared to be his family. The shelves were filled with all kinds of odd mementos. But what really caught Ivan's eye was the beautifully framed design and illustration of what appeared to be a target. It was titled The OnTarget Behaviors and contained 8 components, arranged as a graphic. He had just started to copy them down when Joe came in.

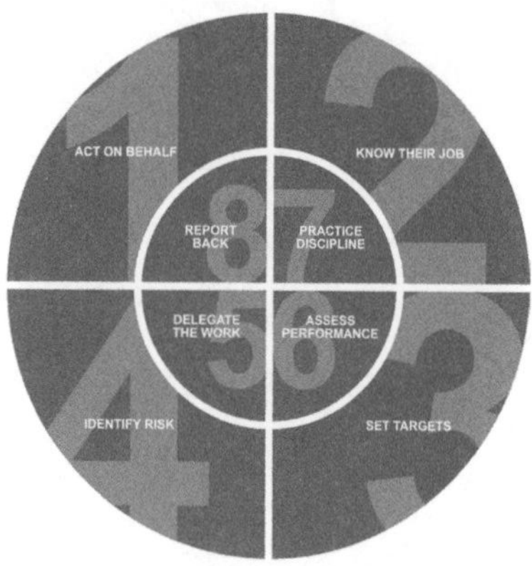

"Ah, Ivan! Thanks for being on time," greeted Joe. "I see you have found the secret to my success—'The OnTarget Behaviors.' Don't bother copying that down. Let me have Jan give you a copy."

At that, Joe walked back to his door and said, "Jan, would you be so kind as to bring Ivan one of our limited-edition prints of 'The OnTarget Behaviors,' please?"

"Certainly, Joe," Ivan heard Jan say. "It will be just a minute—I need to go down to the storeroom for those."

"While she's bringing you that, let's pick up where we left off at the galleria," said Joe. "I know you have a deadline."

"Thanks," said Ivan, nodding his appreciation. "How much time do we have today?"

"Well," said Joe, "I have a conference call at three, and I have an offer for you."

"Oh, really?" joked Ivan. "It's not every day a Fortune 100 CEO makes me an offer. Is it one of those I can't refuse?"

"Oh, nothing like that," said Joe with a chuckle. "The food bank board meets tonight. We're going to consider updating some of our organizational targets, and I thought you might like to observe the behaviors of a good board and how the members look to the future."

"That would be great," Ivan replied. "What time and where?"

"Five o'clock, right here in our boardroom."

"Okay, I accept," agreed Ivan, while mentally giving up his usual Thursday night poker game with the guys. *This is too good to pass up*, he thought.

They heard a subtle knock on the door, which swung gently open. Jan stuck her head in and smiled. "Here is that limited edition, Joe." And then, looking at Ivan, she winked and said, "Get him to autograph it for you—it probably will be worth a million after your story runs!"

They all laughed, and again Ivan marveled at the camaraderie at Allied. *What a cool place*, he thought for at least the third time in the past hour.

"Now, down to business," said Joe, bringing them back to the task at hand. "When we were last together, I was telling you that the OnTarget Team helps boards to begin by focusing on the organization's owners and to understand the board's accountability to the owners. As a result, boards work hard on the right things, ultimately ensuring that benefits accrue to their customers. This is the OnTarget Way."

"Yes," Ivan responded. "Just like on the graphic. I remember that. In fact, we were talking about owners, customers, and clients when we ran out of time. Would that be a good place to start today?"

"Sure," agreed Joe. "Each board must define who its owners are, who its customers are, and where there is overlap. In many nonprofits, this is a whole new and challenging discussion, although it's very easy to distinguish with for-profits.

"For example, here at Allied, many of our customers are also stockholders. So are many employees. However we certainly don't mistake the customer relationship for an owner relationship.

"That makes sense," Ivan agreed. "So the board of a nonprofit defines who its owners are."

Joe nodded approvingly.

"Then what?" asked Ivan.

"Then board members must actively seek out the owners, listen to what they want from the organization, and use that information, along with knowledge of the business and of the business environment, to develop targets," continued Joe. "And that is not always easy to deliver. Remember that the board is accountable to the owners for the work of the organization. So the board is motivated to get it right so that it can report success back to the owners. The challenge in nonprofit organizations is that there is never enough money to do everything, and so the board has to make difficult choices when deciding which targets to achieve."

"Ah, that is the swap with the world that you mentioned last time. When the board identifies which people will get what good and what it's worth," said Ivan.

"Good!" Joe said, nodding enthusiastically, pleased that Ivan was following the conversation.

"Okay," said Ivan. "That helps me understand this thing called 'targets.' Now, may we move on to … I believe they are called staff boundaries?"

"Sure," said Joe. "Just as it sounds, they are boundaries around what staff may do. Here at Allied, we tell folks to 'go fast by letting go.'"

“Say more about that,” encouraged Ivan.

“Did you ever play ‘Mother May I’ when you were a kid?” asked Joe. “Remember that the only way you could advance is after you said, ‘Mother may I?’ It’s limiting, and it’s much like putting a rope on a horse. The horse can’t get away; however it also can’t accomplish much either.

“Instead, using the OnTarget Way, we give the staff a short list of unacceptable ways to conduct themselves as they seek to accomplish our targets. This list is straightforward and pretty commonsense. Jan will have a copy of ours for you when you leave.”

“Let me see if I have this,” Ivan continued, looking back at his notes. “OnTarget Boards know who their owners are. OnTarget Boards meet with these owners regularly to determine what it is that the owners want the organization to accomplish. They make choices on behalf of the owners as to what good the organization is going to do, prioritizing based on what things will cost and who will benefit. They then empower the organization by telling it what it cannot do and letting go of minutiae so the staff can accomplish what the board says is critical. Ultimately the board assesses organizational performance and reports back to the owners."

"Good!" exclaimed Joe again. "You are a quick study."

"But—" began Ivan.

"Hold it," interrupted Joe. "Here at Allied, we say *and*."

"What do you mean?" countered Ivan.

"*But* is a negative word. For example, if I say, 'You look great today, *but*,' what do you immediately think?"

"I think, *What's wrong with how I look?*" answered Ivan.

"Right!" said Joe. "If I say, 'You look great today, *and*,' what do you think?"

"Oh, I get it," said Ivan. "I wonder what the rest of the compliment is."

"Right," Joe said with a nod.

"Okay," said Ivan. "*And* that sounds too simple. If it were that easy, what about Enron and WorldCom and Arthur Andersen and Hollinger International and Bre-Ex? They all had boards too."

"Yes, it is simple," agreed Joe. "That is part of the beauty. The challenge becomes for the board to *make sure* that the organization is accomplishing what it is supposed to and *avoiding* doing what it is not supposed to. My friends at OnTarget call that 'assessing performance.'"

ASSESS PERFORMANCE

Ivan nodded while writing and then circling that phrase.

"Assessing performance—that sounds ominous," ventured Ivan. "Just how I feel when I see a traffic officer—I always look down to make sure I'm not speeding."

"At the same time," Joe continued, "isn't it comforting to know that the officer is there protecting you and others, especially if you have made up your mind to always obey the traffic laws?"

"I see what you mean," said Ivan enthusiastically. "Sure, if the board is watching the organization, and the organization is committed to staying within the boundaries, then there is mutual respect and, I suspect, a sense of empowerment. It is a fair system."

"Like I said," noted Joe, "you are a quick study."

"Well," said Ivan, "does this mean that board members have to be experts in the business? How else can they know all the boundaries and ensure performance?"

"Great question," Joe replied. "Actually, the OnTarget Team does believe that board members must know the business of the organization—and that will happen through regular board education about the business environment. Board members don't, however, need to be experts. Each organization is different, and governing is unique to every organization. The behaviors, however, are consistent across all well-governed, effective boards."

"Whoa, you lost me there, Joe. Go slow; remember I only have a journalism degree," teased Ivan.

"Here, let me come at it this way. Look at your OnTarget graphic. Notice the target with the 8 key behaviors?"

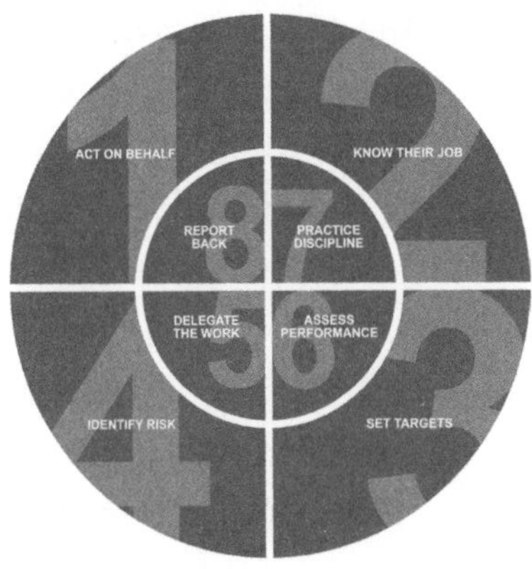

"Sure," said Ivan, nodding.

"Each piece of the target is important. First, you communicate with the owners so that you know what they want. Of course, the board must understand its role and responsibilities. Then, you understand the business internally and externally well enough to set clear targets for the organization and to identify the behaviors the organization must avoid. Then the board delegates the work and checks that it is done. A board must be disciplined about its own performance, and ultimately must be in a position to report back to the owners about a job well done." Joe gestured to each of the 8 pieces as he went around the target.

"Okay," nodded Ivan again. "So while a board must always start by acting on behalf of its owners and even though a board can move through the behaviors logically, no particular behavior is more important than the others, and they are not really mutually exclusive. In fact they can, and should, be done simultaneously and continuously."

"Exactly," replied Joe. "So, as effective board members, we must use the information from the owners, be accountable to them, and report back to them. Based on that information and my knowledge of the business, we must set clear targets for the organization to achieve and we must also identify the risks that are unacceptable. Then we delegate in a way that empowers the staff to do their job and follow-up by rigorously assessing whether the organization has hit the target and avoided the risks. Finally, and above all, the OnTarget Board Member is fully aware of the job of the board and practices discipline in his or her work as a board member."

"So, why are the 8 behaviors depicted as a target? asked Ivan.

"Well," explained Joe, "a target is something to aim for. And in a board's case, the target behaviors are what a well-governed board continually works to achieve. The 8 Indisputable Behaviors are not something that a board can pick up and put down. A good board tries to conduct itself consistently all of the time."

Joe continued, "You link with the owners. You learn the business. You set clear targets. You delegate the work of the organization. You assess organizational performance. You understand your role and are disciplined about it. And you don't stop. You just keep going, and soon things are running pretty well—and you don't stop."

"Now," said Joe, raising his hand to indicate that Ivan should pause for a moment, "because this is a circle, it never ends. Remember our first meeting when we talked about Jim Collins?"

Ivan nodded.

"Jim uses the concept of a flywheel. You push and push and push and push, and you get one turn of the flywheel. And you don't stop. You push and push and push and push, and you get a second turn. And you don't stop. You push and push, and you get a third turn. And you don't stop. Pretty soon the flywheel is turning freely, and you don't stop."

Joe sat back in his chair and simply gazed quietly at Ivan.

Ivan looked at Joe, then at the diagram, and then back at Joe. For one of the few times in his journalistic career, he was mesmerized. He felt as if he had just earned an MBG: a master of board governance. Then his journalism degree kicked in, and he opened his mouth to say, "Come on … it just can't be that easy." But then there was another discreet knock on the office door. And, sure enough, it was followed by Jan with her ever-present—and obviously real—smile.

"Joe, you'll need a couple of minutes to freshen up before your three o'clock," Jan said. "Shall I take care of Ivan for you?"

"Sure, that would be great," agreed Joe. "And Jan, will you be sure and show Ivan the boardroom where the food bank board will be meeting tonight? He's going to join us for this evening's meeting."

"Of course, Joe," Jan replied. "It will be a pleasure. Mr. John, will you please follow me?"

"Call me Ivan," Ivan said automatically as they both laughed.

Before Ivan left, he said, "Joe, this is impressive, but … I mean, and … I still have a couple of questions."

"Of course," Joe said. "That is your business. There will be a few minutes tonight to wrap up. Now, if you will go with Jan, she will show you the boardroom."

As Ivan left the office with Jan, he jotted the following in his notebook:

- OnTarget Board Members
  - Seek their owners: Who are they? What do they want?
  - Set targets and identify risks
  - Delegate and set boundaries
  - Assess performance
  - Report back to and are accountable to the owners
  - Know their job and are disciplined
  - Consistently work to govern well using all of the behaviors simultaneously
  - And they keep going

Chapter 7

The Boardroom

"WOW, AND I THOUGHT Joe's office was nice," Ivan said as he walked into the Allied boardroom. "This place looks like something from *Star Wars*."

Again Jan laughed. "Joe is a big believer in technology. He uses all of these tools to stay in touch with the board, the employees, and our satellite offices."

Ivan continued to marvel. "I've never seen a completely round board table before. This is like something out of King Arthur. I feel as if I should sing a chorus of *Camelot*."

Jan continued to laugh. "Oh, Ivan, you are so fun. Actually, the idea of a round table is pretty central to Joe's OnTarget Way of doing things. Whoever gets to the room first picks any seat they want, and then others fill in. That way, there is no 'head' of the table and no "power" seats. Power is shared, and leadership shifts based on need and expertise. Remember, OnTarget board members use their best talents and expertise for the good of the owners and the customers. Hierarchical games and jockeying for position do not go over well at Allied or, for that matter, at the food bank or on any board Joe is associated with."

"Okay, that's it," Ivan said. "Where do I get an application to work here?"

"Oh, we rarely advertise, Ivan. All the best people want to come to Allied. And remember our superstar watch list? We really do keep a good group of next-generation talent. Besides," she whispered conspiratorially, "I think Joe has his eye on you already."

"Hmmm, buttering me up so my article will be good?" teased Ivan.

"Not at all," Jan retorted. "Just giving you the benefit of my wisdom—acquired over many years, I might add. Joe rarely gives interviews, you know. And for him to invite you to the board meeting tonight is quite unusual."

"Just kidding," Ivan responded. "I know when I'm being handed a line. You all have been strictly professional here."

"Apology accepted," said Jan with a forgiving look.

"Say, what is this? Secret information?" said Ivan as he noticed several official-looking notebooks titled "Allied Board Policies."

"Go ahead and take a look and," Jan continued, "while you are doing that, I will get you another glass of water."

The first thing Ivan noticed about the Allied board policies was that the notebook was only about an inch thick. *That's not many policies for a billion-a-year company*, thought Ivan. He noticed that the notebook was divided into four parts: targets, boundaries, board authority, and delegation to the CEO.

KNOW THEIR JOB

There is something to ask about, thought Ivan. *Board authority. That sounds interesting.*

"Here is that water, Ivan," said Jan as she came back into the room. "You'll be learning a lot more about board authority and discipline at the meeting tonight. You're welcome to camp here until the meeting at five, or I can give you a parking pass to the garage so that you can come up the elevator later on."

"I tell you what ... can I do both?" inquired Ivan. "Let me check my e-mail and work from here for a bit, and then I'll go grab a bite and be back in time for the meeting tonight."

"Sure, although if you are going to eat anyway, may I suggest our cafeteria in the mezzanine? You'll probably see Joe there between four and four thirty."

"Joe eats in a cafeteria?" burst out Ivan. "Come on ... you're pulling my leg."

Jan laughed again. "Ivan, I am going to be sore tonight from all of this laughing! Of course Joe eats in the cafeteria. In fact, he insists that we all do on a regular basis. He says, 'Leaders must be visible and approachable.' He tries to know every employee here at corporate by name, and he even knows many of their family members' names. He speaks to every new employee personally and tells all new executives that the employees will never care how much they know until those employees know how much the executive cares."

"Wow, I'm going to have to do a CEO piece on Joe after this board piece."

"Well, that would take a book," Jan replied. "Joe is perhaps the most complete individual I have ever met. He utilizes the OnTarget Behaviors in the boardroom at both Allied and the food bank, in the office, and at home. To paraphrase an old comedian, with Joe, 'What you see is what you get!'"

Ivan joined Jan in laughing out loud. Again he shook his head. "What a dream organization."

"Yes, Joe believes in being effective. Results matter. Of course, how we get there is important, nevertheless delivering results is what ultimately counts. He simply models this behavior for all of us.

"He also reminds us that just as the board is accountable to the owners, so are we accountable to the board and to each other. It sounds trite, I know, but Allied really is a high-performance team."

After Jan left, Ivan wrote the following in his notebook:

- Shared power, round board table
- A good set of board policies addresses four board concerns:
    - Targets
    - Boundaries
    - Board authority
    - Delegation to the CEO
- Results matter
- The OnTarget Behaviors apply in many situations

Chapter 8

The Cafeteria

IVAN FOUND THE CAFETERIA more by smell than by directions. On par with his experience so far at Allied, he was immediately impressed. The place was spotless, the employees were courteous to the extreme, and the food looked delicious.

When he reached the checkout line, he took out his wallet, but there was no checker, only an electronic scanner. While he was looking at the scanner and wondering what to do, he heard a familiar voice.

"Ivan, you can be my guest," said Susan as she swiped her ID badge.

"Hi, Susan," greeted Ivan. "Thanks, but ... oops ... I mean, thanks, *and* I really should pay for my own meal. My editors don't want me to take gifts from the folks I write about, you know."

Susan laughed gently at the correction. "Ahh, you have had the but-and discussion."

Ivan nodded.

"Tell you what, Ivan; I'll have Jan bill you for the meal. Will that keep you in compliance with your limitations?"

"It will, and by the way, do you have anyone to eat with?" asked Ivan.

"Come on over. Joe's telling stories," said Susan, pointing with her head.

Balancing his tray, iced tea and notebook, Ivan followed Susan to her table. "Say, Susan, why are you still here? Don't you go home at four?"

"Oh, Allied is big on flex time and family time. I live about twenty miles out, and traffic is murder this time of day. So I come in around ten and generally leave about seven or so. That way, my commute is twenty minutes instead of an hour and twenty minutes. I really cherish the mornings with my kids, fixing breakfast and getting them off to school, and my husband enjoys having them to himself at dinner. I get home in time for baths, snacks, and stories. It is a great benefit. And," Susan continued, "if I need to be gone for a school event, I simply pop in a bit earlier in the day. After all, results matter, and I work really hard to make sure I don't disappoint my team members."

"Ah, 'results matter,'" Ivan said. "What a great culture you have here at Allied. Surely it can't be this good top to bottom?"

"Oh, like any large organization, we make a mistake now and then, but we work really hard at hiring attitude and teaching skills. That way, we know that everyone buys into our principles and values. And really, Ivan, it starts at the top. Here—sit here and listen to Joe."

Even though he was surrounded by several (mostly young) employees, Joe took time to nod and wave as Ivan caught his eye, and then he continued with his story. "That was in the early days," Joe was saying. "Once I understood the role of the board and how it could become accountable and effective and began modeling that behavior here, it didn't take long for the Allied board to come on board." Joe laughed at his pun.

Ivan quietly took out his ever-present reporter's spiral. *This could be good,* he thought, *and no one said it was off the record.*

Joe continued, "As you know, it's easy to come up with activities, however it's harder to define a target. So many board members want to help the staff by telling them how to do things or feel like they have to put staff through their paces. An OnTarget Board Member works smarter on the big picture stuff, long term priorities, and it pays off.

"Think of it this way: here at Allied, the board describes the destination for us, and we decide whether to fly, go by boat, drive, or even invent a new transportation system. They tell us how much they are willing to invest in the journey and when they would like to get there. As long as we don't go outside the boundaries that they set for us in advance we are free to use the best talent of the organization to get us there."

"Joe," one of the twentysomethings at the table interrupted, "can you give us a concrete example of this type of leadership?"

"Sure, Stephen. Let me give you two. As you know, the food bank board is going to meet here in about thirty minutes.

Many of you have helped on their food drives. In fact, Allied was their single largest contributor of actual food last year."

Ivan watched the high fives go around the room.

Joe continued, "The board of the food bank has said that our business is about alleviating hunger. In fact, it is our expectation that no one in Chamton goes hungry. And our official board-stated target is exactly that. We have also clearly identified a few strategic priorities within that target. And the rest is up to our CEO. She is empowered to further define that target, determining reasonable subsidiary targets, which operationalize our higher-level goals.

"Now, *how* that is done is not the board's work; rather it is the work of our CEO to interpret what that target means and how she will get to the target. As a board member, I can offer advice—which, by definition, she can take or leave—volunteer to work a drive, even burn the hot dogs."

At this, everyone groaned. Ivan decided it must be an inside joke. *The power of stories*, he thought.

"When I do volunteer," Joe continued, "I have the same status as anyone else. The CEO is free to accept or reject my suggestions. She is accountable to the entire board, never to me personally. So she is free to serve hot dogs or hamburgers at the annual share-your-brown-bag hunger day. In fact, she doesn't even have to have a hunger day."

Joe paused and looked around the room before he continued. "My second example is a boundaries example. Stephen, since you're in HR, you will especially appreciate this one."

Stephen nodded, pleased that the CEO would remember him and his position in the company. Ivan could see Joe's charisma coming through, and he was impressed that it was so genuine.

"Again, as you know, our board has said that we may not operate without written personnel policies that set out rules for staff. This is because the board values ethical treatment of staff and doesn't want you to be working in confusing conditions.

But they don't get involved in writing those rules or even approving them. They leave it to staff to further define what those rules look like, do the research, decide on the content, design the format, communicate those rules to staff, and design the evaluations, right down to the color of the paper used. The board's role is then to make sure that the organization has complied with a reasonable interpretation of that policy. Does that help?"

Stephen again nodded and said, "Sure that helps a lot. Thanks!"

At this, Joe looked again at Ivan and said, "Well, speaking of the food bank board, I guess we better get upstairs. Our chair starts on time, and it wouldn't look good for me to be late in my own building."

Everyone laughed, but they quieted when Joe held up his hand. "Hey, everyone, I want to make sure you have a chance to greet Ivan John. Ivan is my guest tonight and is writing a story about boards. You all will want to read it, I'm sure. Ivan, thanks for being here this evening."

As the room turned to look at him and give polite applause, Ivan waved his hand and gave Joe a thumbs-up sign, and then he stood up as Joe headed over to him.

"Are you ready to go up?" Joe queried.

"Sure," said Ivan. "Susan, for the second time today, thanks. And don't forget to bill me for the dinner."

As Ivan carried his tray over to the counter, he wondered again about the Allied culture. *Unbelievable*, he thought. *I've never even met the CEO over at the paper, and here this guy is hanging out at the cafeteria. Unbelievable!*

While he was walking, he quickly scribbled the following in his notebook:

- Ask for the dinner; don't design the menu
- Board sets strategic priorities or targets
- Results matter
- Set the target; delegate achievement within boundaries

Chapter 9

The Food Bank Board Meeting

AS THEY REACHED THE boardroom, Joe said to Ivan, "I hope you don't mind sitting at the table with us. I took the liberty of calling the board chair, Nanci Oreo, earlier today and shared that I had invited you. She was thrilled and suggested that you consider yourself part of the group."

"Well, Joe, that's very kind of you," Ivan replied, "but I do want to stay objective here. After all, we wouldn't want anyone saying I took it too easy on you."

Joe laughed. "Oh, that's okay, Ivan. I think the food bank folks are just happy about the publicity they might receive. The more people who know about us, the better."

With that, Joe opened the door and ushered Ivan in.

As they took their seats at the round table, Ivan was struck with how organized everything was. Every board member had an agenda at their place. Each also had a notebook that appeared to contain background information on each of the items. It was obvious that all of the members had taken time to review the notebook, because each one was full of sticky notes and turned pages. There was a table at the back with coffee, tea, water, and snacks. Classical music wafted from the speakers set in the ceiling. Around the perimeter of the room were a series of easels with flip charts and markers.

PRACTICE DISCIPLINE

No sooner had they sat down than the music faded and the individual that Ivan presumed was Ms. Oreo called the meeting to order.

"Ladies and gentlemen, thanks for being on time tonight. First, I want to thank Joe Victor for allowing us to use the Allied boardroom again this evening. And, Joe, thanks too for the music and refreshments. Now," she continued, "I understand you have a guest this evening."

"Yes, Madam Chair, I do," Joe assented. "Everyone, I would like you to meet Ivan John. I'm sure that many of you recognize his name. Ivan writes for the *Sunday News*. He is doing a story on boards of directors here in greater Chamton and, as part of that, has been meeting with me and others. I invited him this evening so that he can see how the best board in Chamton operates."

At this, everyone at the table chuckled, and a few even clapped and hooted.

"Of course," Joe continued, "I've shared with Ivan many of our governance principles and told him that tonight we will be working on our target policies. Fair warning, though: what you say here tonight can and will be held against you in the *Sunday News*."

Again there was a round of laughter.

"Thanks for that introduction," said the chair, reasserting her control over the meeting. "Everyone, please take a minute to go around the table and tell Mr. John just a bit about yourselves."

As the board members introduced themselves, Ivan was struck with the caliber of the group. Each of the board members was successful in his or her own way, and yet here they were on a weeknight, taking time to talk about food for the less fortunate. It was clear that the group members liked each other, but, more than that, they clearly had a passion for the mission of the food bank.

After the introductions were complete, the chair again took on the captaincy of the meeting.

"As we begin this evening, I would like to ask for agreement that Jordan be our meeting monitor tonight and evaluate our performance during the meeting against the board authority policy titled 'Governing Style'[2], specifically clause 1 regarding group responsibility and clause 3 regarding discipline. I spoke with Jordan earlier to ensure that she is familiar with the policy and prepared to monitor."

PRACTICE DISCIPLINE

[2] See Appendix 4

All hands were raised.

"Thank you, Jordan."

Nanci continued, "Are there any deletions or additions to the agenda?[3] No? Good. I will remind you that we are scheduled until 8 this evening, and I promise to do my best to get you out of here on time."

"Hear! Hear!" several of the members agreed.

Without missing a beat, the chair continued, "The first item is the Required Approval Agenda. A submission for a request for funding from the Chamton Community Foundation requires board approval. Clearly they're not using the OnTarget way," Nanci joked. "We've received a compliance report from our CEO identifying how this funding is aligned with our targets and priorities and how it will not go outside our boundaries. Are there any questions? I will accept a motion that the interpretations are reasonable and that the data satisfies us of compliance."

Following the motion and the seconding, the chair called the question. Everyone voted in the affirmative.

Ivan looked at his watch. Barely fifteen minutes had elapsed, and already the board had dealt very efficiently with a number of items. *Maybe I will get out of here by 8*, he thought while writing down "Use Required Approval Agenda." His Friday deadline had been extended to Saturday mid-morning, but there was still a lot of work to do.

Once again, the chair spoke. "Has everyone received and read the 'Treatment of Clients' compliance report?" All heads nodded.[4]

---

[3] See Appendix 3

[4] See Appendixes 5 and 6

Then the chair asked two questions separately: "Has the CEO convincingly demonstrated the reasonableness of her interpretations of the policy?" and "Is there sufficient evidence to convince you that this policy has been complied with?"

A healthy discussion ensued, with both questions being answered in the affirmative by all board members. It was then recorded in the minutes that the board had received the staff compliance report for the policy titled "Treatment of Clients" and accepted that the CEO had convincingly demonstrated her interpretations and submitted data that proved compliance. This was also recorded by the board's secretary on a separate tracking sheet to be used, along with other similar decisions, at year-end for the performance appraisal of the executive director.

"As you know," the chair continued, "this evening's meeting will focus on decision making about our target policies. We have been collecting data throughout the past six months, and tonight we will review all that we have read and heard. Based on these data, the board will decide whether to amend our target policies.

"I have prepared for you a set of documents, which was included in your board packet. I know that all of you have read it, as you always do. You have seen all the material already. I have simply gathered it together so that we are all working from the same documents. To set the stage for our discussion, let me give you an overview of the documents and take you through a bit of a chronology of our past six months of target work. You can follow along on the yellow cover sheet. Mr. John, I have an extra set of documents for you to follow along. I think you will find them interesting.

"Our current target policy, reviewed and adopted by us last June, is in tab 1 of your board binder.[5] Behind that policy is the latest report from the CEO on the achievement of our target.[6] You will remember that when the board accepted that report, we asked ourselves two questions: 'Have we targeted the right groups? What are the contributing factors to hunger and food insufficiency?' The answers to these will be our board education priority topics.

"The next document in your package is the notes from our leader's meeting in September, as well as from our meeting with representatives from the City Council, the Interfaith Council of Chamton, and the Coalition of Social Service Agencies. The questions we asked in that meeting were as follows:

- Who is most at risk for going hungry?
- What is the impact of the current level of people going hungry?
- What are the long-term solutions your organization is using to address hunger?

---

[5] See Appendix 7

[6] See Appendix 8

- How important is the issue of hunger to our constituents?

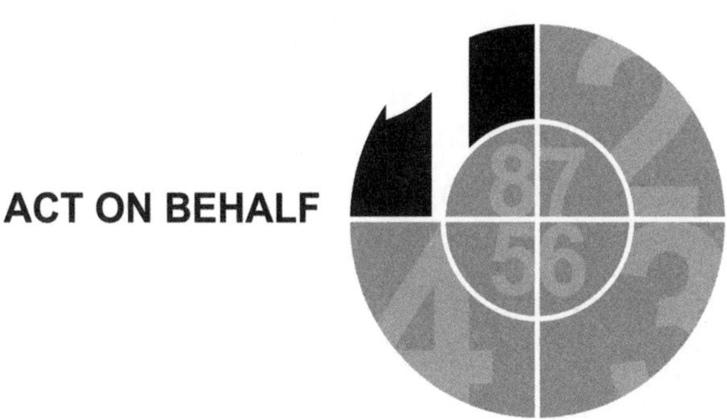

"In November, we held six neighborhood focus group meetings. The summary of those meetings is your next document. The focus for those meetings was this set of questions:

- What would you consider to be an adequate supply of food?
- What does a person need to ensure an adequate supply of food?
- What are the barriers to having an adequate supply of food?

"The last document in your package contains the results of our organization's latest annual survey of food bank clients.

"There is a lot of material here, rich with information that we need. I know you all have read everything. I suggest that we take the next thirty minutes to meet in small groups to digest and analyze the information.

"Why don't we have three groups? Mr. John, please feel welcome to join one of the groups as well. Each group will take one of the documents. Jordan, your group can discuss the neighborhood focus groups summary; Pat, your group can take the annual survey; and Kathy, you take the document from our September leader's meeting.

"Here are the guiding questions for your group:

- What words, or data, caught your attention?
- What is in the document that is worrisome?
- What is surprising?
- What did you read that is validating?
- What are the specific points that would have an impact on our organization?
- What values do you see reflected in this document?
- Which ones are not there?
- What do you recommend to the board?

"Please take notes from your group discussion, and be prepared to make your points back to the larger group after the thirty minutes are up."

Ivan was quickly asked to join one of the small groups and immediately found himself to be part of an interesting and lively discussion about hunger. He wisely didn't enter the discussion, because he had not read the documents. By listening to the others, he became vastly more educated about the issues causing hunger and the different values about hunger in the community. He wondered how the board was going to make a decision.

After thirty minutes, the board chair called the groups back to order and asked for a presentation from each small group.

"You have fifteen minutes each to report back," the chair said. "At the end of each group's presentation, there will be questions for clarification. At the end of all the presentations, we will have a brief stretch break and then reconvene for board decision making.

"Now, who would like to go first? Kathy, is your group ready to go? Okay, let's hear what your thoughts are from the September meeting."

Kathy said, "Well, Charlie took the notes while we were talking, so I'll defer to him, in case I might miss something."

"Thanks Kathy", said Charlie. "All the board members in our group were also in attendance at that meeting in September, so we used our own personal impressions of the meeting as well as the meeting summary notes. In summary, we heard the following:

- Children living in poverty, new immigrants, and people with disabilities are those most at risk for going hungry.
- Children living in poverty and going hungry are also eating less nutritious food. They are therefore at increased risk of obesity and other health problems in the future.
- Hunger has a negative impact on children's ability to learn.
- Other organizations are focusing in two areas to end hunger in this city: lobbying state government to increase the minimum wage and basic welfare assistance rates and removing the barriers to the use of food stamps.
- Donations to food banks are down nationally due to increased giving to victims of international disasters."

The reports from the small groups filled the next forty-five minutes. Ivan observed the board members listening intently to each other and taking notes. Board members heard more about the barriers experienced by people applying to use food stamps, as well as more detail about immigrants and children experiencing food insecurity and hunger. A theme that emerged was that the board was almost completely "OnTarget" with the current list of outcomes that the organization should be achieving, although there were a few potential changes to the targets.

At the break, Ivan spotted Joe across the room and gave him an appreciative grin. Ivan realized he was getting considerably more access and exposure to his topic than most interviewees would allow.

After the break, the chair reconvened the board and asked for proposals from individual board members regarding amending the board target policies. Jordan proposed that the board specify "people with disabilities and new immigrants" in policy 1 by adding a policy 1(a) to further clarify "those who are most vulnerable will include new immigrants and people with disabilities."

"I second that motion," added Kathy.

The board members entered into a hearty debate about this proposal. When it appeared the discussion was winding down, the chair asked, "All those in favor of amending our policy?" Seven hands were raised. "All those opposed to amending the policies?" Two hands went up. "We have a decision then to amend our target policy as proposed. Well done, everyone. I think that those who we represent around this table would agree that we considered all the information, views, and values in making this decision.

"Now let's hear from our meeting monitor. Jordan, how did we do?"

"I observed our behavior this evening and compared it with the Governing Style policy, clauses 1 and 3," Jordan said. "Based on my earlier conversation with Nanci, our chair, and understanding her interpretations of group responsibility and discipline, I report to you the following:

- The board demonstrated its own responsibility for excellence in governing through the chair's design and execution of the meeting agenda, which both accomplished our stated meeting outcomes and included everyone in the discussion.
- All board members were on time for the meeting and present for the full meeting. We had 100 percent attendance.
- As I listened in to the small-group discussions during the meeting, it was evident from both the quality of the comments and the state of people's board packages, which were all highlighted and dog-eared, that everyone came to this meeting thoroughly prepared.

"So, on a scale of 1 to 10, I would assess our performance at very close to a 10 for tonight's meeting. Well done, everyone."

PRACTICE DISCIPLINE

Ivan leaned over and whispered to Joe, “May I get a copy of that board assessment report?”

“Sure,” Joe whispered back. “I’ll have Jan e-mail it to you first thing tomorrow. We use almost the same one at Allied.”

“Okay. Thanks, Jordan,” the chair said. “I look forward to reporting on this meeting in our next community newsletter along with our new version of our target policies.”

“By my watch, it is 7:58, and we’re ready to adjourn a couple of minutes early. Joe, thanks again for the use of the room. I declare us adjourned. Drive safely everyone.”

As the meeting broke up, several of the members stopped by to say good-bye to Joe and to thank Ivan for being there.

When Nanci approached, Ivan said, "Ms. Oreo, that was one of the best meetings I have ever observed. Is there any way at all that I can get a few minutes of your time to talk about how you learned to do that?"

"Well," said Nanci, "I really can't stay tonight. I have children at home that I have to put to bed on a school night. Tell you what, though—I will meet you at the Starbucks over on Main Street for a half hour in the morning at eight o'clock."

Although he was groaning on the inside at the prospect of an eight o'clock meeting, Ivan put on his game face and nodded. "See you there, and thanks," he said.

While he had a minute alone, Ivan wrote the following in his notebook:

- Seek owner input and use it
- Stay on track; be disciplined about the board's work
- Get the board to discuss big picture issues in a meaningful way and process difficult information
- The board must assess organizational performance
- The board must assess its own performance

Chapter 10

The Parking Garage

"THAT BOARD MEETING WAS a wonderful experience," said Ivan as he and Joe walked to their cars. "I learned more than I ever expected."

"Good," said Joe, beaming. "I always try to amaze. So, after all of that, are there any other questions I might answer for you?"

"Well ..." hesitated Ivan.

"Go ahead," encouraged Joe.

"Well," continued Ivan, "if good governance is this easy, why aren't all boards doing it as well?"

"Whoa, Ivan. You said 'easy.' I would like to suggest that it is not easy. It is straightforward and, for an accomplished practitioner, perhaps even simple, but it is not easy," replied Joe.

"What is the difference?"

"Well, do you golf or ride a bike?" asked Joe.

"Sure. In fact, riding is one of my favorite activities. There are some great trails here in Chamton."

"So would you say riding is easy?" queried Joe, and then he followed up his question with another. "And how about *learning* to ride?"

Joe went on while Ivan was pondering. "When my son was little, we started him on a tricycle and then switched to a little bike with training wheels."

"Sure," agreed Ivan. "We pretty much all started that way."

"Right," said Joe with a nod. "When he was about age five or so, we took the training wheels off, and I spent most of a Saturday running along beside him, holding on to the saddle to give him confidence. All at once, it just clicked for him, and he began to ride on his own."

Again Ivan nodded, knowing that Joe was going somewhere but still not sure he was tracking with him.

Joe continued, "There were a few crashes, most not serious, and along the way he grew from a twelve-inch bike to a sixteen-inch and then a twenty-inch; he went from no gears to twenty-one speeds.

"Now," Joe said, "let me ask again. Is bike riding easy?"

"I get it," said Ivan. "Depending on where you are in your development, and depending on what level of performance you want, riding can be hard. The concept of riding, though, is pretty simple, and almost everyone with a modicum of physical ability can do it to some degree."

"Right!" exclaimed Joe. "Being on a board is like that. Most folks start out, learn as they go, have a few crashes, and, depending on their desired level of performance, muddle through. To govern well, though, requires some skills and some training. With some practice, the behaviors look pretty easy."

PRACTICE DISCIPLINE

Joe took a deep breath. "It gets even more difficult in publicly elected bodies like city councils, school boards, and special district boards. Watch the city council on TV some time, and observe them turn themselves inside out to treat citizens like owners on a customer issue." Joe shook his head despairingly.

"I'm not sure I follow that," said Ivan. "How do you mean?"

"Remember when we talked about owners and customers? A citizen buys a house, pays taxes, and lives in the community and so considers himself an owner of the community, and that is a good thing. Then their garbage doesn't get picked up or the pothole on their street doesn't get fixed, and so they run down to the city council to complain. They are now being a customer.

"At that point, the council should stop and ask themselves, 'What is our target here? What have we said about this from an outcome perspective? Is this an owner issue or a customer issue?' but they almost never have this discussion. Instead they start talking about a new pothole program or adding garbage trucks. Sometimes they engage in this conversation because they haven't clearly delegated to the CEO. However sometimes this is what I call the “show factor” and happens when elected directors bow to subtle pressure with the sole purpose of getting attention, and being on show. Think of how a city council meeting is physically set up. It doesn’t look anything like our round board table, does it?”

“Let me say it another way. I own an SUV to haul all the kids and their toys around.” Joe continued, “I also own some of that company’s stock. Occasionally I take my vehicle in to have it serviced. I get great service, but it’s clear that I’m there as a customer, not as an owner, not even as a significant owner. If I asked for special pricing or even special treatment because of my stock ownership, I would be laughed out the door.

“What happens at city council and at school board of trustee meetings is that everyone wants to be treated as an owner and never as a customer, no matter what the item is. Issues such as appropriate dress codes for students, what kind of police cars officers drive, and whether garbage is picked up by hand or by automated truck all get hotly debated by the board or council, but these same groups rarely ever talk about educational outcomes, and the council rarely talks about quality of life for the community at large. They mire themselves in minutiae while big things go unaddressed.”

“But, Joe,” said Ivan, “people want their elected representatives to listen to them. Isn’t that what democracy is all about?”

“Yes, Ivan, you are right. The challenge lies in whom they listen to and what they talk about. Can you imagine the board of General Motors or Ford or Toyota getting involved at the level of discussing what color of cars should be sold next year?”

KNOW THEIR JOB

"Of course not," agreed Ivan, still shaking his head. "But we're not talking about a major corporation; we're talking about a town or a school."

"Right again," said Joe. "Tell me, which is more important, making cars or educating kids?"

"Well …" began Ivan.

"If you will pardon the pun, let me change gears again," Joe said earnestly. "All boards have limited resources, right? Money is the most commonly thought-of resource, but time and energy also figure in. With limited resources, and especially focusing on time as a resource, what issues should a board tackle?"

"Well, I suppose whatever is most important," ventured Ivan.

"Exactly!" exclaimed Joe. "So, whether we're talking about a large multi-national corporation or the city council or the food bank, the board should spend its resources and its time on the most critical item, which is the future of the organization and the benefit the organization brings to the world, not the mechanisms to accomplish things. That is what the staff is for. That is why there are professional managers. That is why there is a service department. That is what the food bank group did tonight."

"Okay, okay," said Ivan, smiling and waving his hands. "Point made; point taken. I get it."

"Sorry to be so forceful there, Ivan," said Joe. "It's such a soapbox for me. Government is critical to the delivery of democracy, and it frustrates me to watch elected officials pander to the media and dissidents. Thanks for hearing me out on that one."

"Say," added Joe, "that quote about pandering won't show up in the article, will it?"

"No," laughed Ivan. "Consider that off the record. And Joe," continued Ivan, "thanks again for all of your time. I learned a lot."

"It was my pleasure, Ivan," returned Joe. "Be sure and stop by sometime. I would like to stay in touch with you."

As Ivan opened his car door, he took time to write the following in his reporter's notebook:

- Money and time are resources
- Deal with the big issues

- Good governance is simple but not easy
- Delegate
- Distinguish between owners and customers

Chapter 11

Starbucks

"MAN, THESE ONTARGET BOARD Members sure seem to get by on less sleep than I do," Ivan groaned to himself the next morning as he pulled into Starbucks.

True to her word, Nanci walked in right at 8 o'clock. Ivan noticed that the counter clerk began pouring Nanci's coffee as soon as she came through the door.

"Hey, you must be a regular," said Ivan as Nanci joined him.

"Oh, I generally hit the drive-through," answered Nanci. "That's my daughter. She goes to college around the corner. She works here to get her spending money. Unfortunately, I don't get her discount, and I always leave a big tip."

"Ahh," said Ivan, smiling. "Sort of pay me now or pay me later?"

"You got it," agreed Nanci. "And while I certainly don't mean to rush you, I do have to leave at eight thirty to get to another appointment."

"Of course," said Ivan as he gathered up his spiral. "If I may, I'd like to compliment you on the meeting again. I cover a fair number of meetings for the paper when other reporters are on vacation, and I must say, that was one of the best. What I noticed was that everyone had policies available to them;

they were written down and referred to frequently throughout the meeting."

At this, Nanci nodded and said simply, "Well, that is the OnTarget Way, you know."

"Sure," agreed Ivan. "I guess what I want to know is how, as board chair, you keep the discipline you need to get everyone to do all of that."

"It does take discipline," said Nanci after taking a sip of her latte.

PRACTICE DISCIPLINE

"The fact is that when we recruit new board members, we share right up front our expectations, including requirements for attendance, participation, preparedness, orientation, and ongoing behaviors. Frankly we have had a few individuals decline to serve as a result. Still, what my experience tells me is that if people know in advance what is expected of them and experience everyone being held accountable, they quickly get up to speed and behave accordingly.

"So setting expectations is the key?" queried Ivan.

"I would say so," said Nanci with a nod. "Unless they are reading a mystery novel, adults like to know what is coming. By telling them in advance how we do things—and, just as importantly, why we do them that way—we remove the ambiguity. At that point, everything is on the table. My job as chair is to make sure the board is doing its job, the job we said we would do. By the way, my job as board chair is not to supervise or instruct the Executive Director because she works for the whole board."

"The food bank board members expect the board meetings to be structured in such a way that the agenda items are clear, material is circulated in advance, and everyone participates at the board meeting. We also expect people to be prepared and on time for the meeting; we're really sticklers for those things."

"Okay," Ivan said, nodding thoughtfully. "I can see that. I guess it is like Starbucks or McDonald's. No matter where I am in Chamton—or anywhere else, for that matter—I know what I'm going to experience when I come through the door. That makes it comfortable for me, and so I don't ever worry about stopping in."

"Great example," said Nanci with a smile. "And to stay with that thought for a minute, the food bank board members would actually be quite concerned if the meeting was not disciplined. It would be as if you walked into a Starbucks and everything was out of place, the coffee was cold, and the Internet didn't work. You would be questioning what in the world was going on."

'Whoa," said Ivan. "Don't even suggest that. I will have nightmares for a week."

Nanci laughed and after a little more conversation, said, "To keep us on track, I have only a few more minutes left. Do you have any other questions?"

Ivan flipped back through his spiral and looked at his notes from the previous night. "No, you have been most gracious. On the unlikely chance that I need some clarification later, may I call you?"

"Sure," agreed Nanci. "And, Ivan, thanks again for using the food bank in your story. I'm really looking forward to the *Sunday News* this week."

"Speaking of the *Sunday News*, I better zip on over there and get to work. This is going to be a challenging story to keep within my space limitations," said Ivan as he put his spiral and pen away.

"Once again, thanks for your time this morning," he said as they stood and shook hands.

As he walked out the door, he couldn't help but grin as he saw Nanci's daughter serve her mom a fresh coffee for the road.

As soon as Ivan sat down at his desk, he added a few final notes in his reporter's notebook:

- Use the board's policies at board meetings
- The role of the chair is to keep the board on target
- Board members need to know their jobs, in advance
- Discipline is expected, not just hoped for
- Board Chair is not the supervisor of the CEO

Chapter 12

The Newsroom

"HEY, IVAN. WHAT'S UP? What are you doing here so early?" asked his cube mate shortly after nine that morning.

"Oh, I have that big story on boards due in the morning," Ivan replied, "and I'm just trying to get going on it."

"Man, must be a great story for you to get in here this time of day."

"You know, it really is," said Ivan with a smile. "At least a really good story. And I've already had my Starbucks."

Collecting his notes and quotes, Ivan started by putting all his critical points in a Word document. He saved it on his desktop machine as "Great Boards Story—Key Points First Draft." Once the list was created in its draft form, he printed it out and began to study it for common themes and redundancies. He began to cut and paste, and then he saved this new document as "Great Boards—Key Points." When it was done, he printed it out and thumbtacked it to his corkboard.

GREAT BOARDS—KEY POINTS

There is an OnTarget Way.

There are 8 Indisputable Behaviors of OnTarget Board Members:

OnTarget board members...

#1 Act on behalf of their owners

- √ Seek their owners: Who are they? What do they want?
- √ Understanding who their owner are and act on their behalf
- √ Seek owner input and use it
- √ Distinguish between owners and customers

#2 Know their job

- √ Know their legal duties
- √ Understand the business of the organization
- √ Board members need to know their jobs, in advance

#3 Set targets

- √ Set targets for the organization to achieve
- √ Results matter
- √ Focus on the big picture
- √ Start with the big things first
- √ Make choices about targets
- √ Write down the targets
- √ Boards need good board education to be able to set targets

#4 Identify the risks

- √ Say what is unacceptable
- √ Establish boundaries on staff actions
- √ Freedom through limits

- √ Write down the boundaries

#5 Delegate the work

- √ Ask for the dinner; don't design the menu
- √ Delegate to staff achievement of targets and work within boundaries
- √ Stay out of staff decisions

#6 Assess performance

- √ Assess whether the targets were achieved
- √ Assess whether the staff stayed within the boundaries

#7 Practice discipline

- √ Good board policy addresses four issues:
  - Targets
  - Boundaries
  - Board authority
  - Delegation to the CEO
- √ Stay on track; be disciplined about the board's work
- √ Assess the board's own performance
- √ Money and time are resources
- √ This is simple, not easy
- √ Use the board's policies at board meetings
- √ The role of the chair is to keep the board on target
- √ Discipline is expected, not just hoped for
- √ Consistently work to govern well using all of the behaviors, often simultaneously

#8 Report back to their owners

- √ Boards are accountable to the owner

A good start, Ivan thought, and then he quoted that early management guru, Mary Poppins: *Well begun is half done!*

Laughing at himself, he grabbed a bottle of water from the machine and came back to the task at hand. Selecting "New Blank Document," he began to type.

"Hey, Ivan!"

Ivan jumped and looked up into the eyes of his editor.

"Yes, sir. Sorry, sir. I was really far away there, wasn't I?"

"Yep. Just wanted to remind you that I want that board story on my desk first thing in the morning."

"You got it, boss."

Later that night, Ivan attached his final copy to an e-mail and hit "Send."

Leaning back in his chair, he beamed and said to no one in particular, "I think it's a good story—very much OnTarget!"

Chapter 13

The Story

INDISPUTABLY GREAT BOARDS—RIGHT HERE IN CHAMTON!

THEY LURK LARGELY OUT of view. With little fanfare, these groups impact our lives in ways most of us never know. Unseen and certainly unheralded, boards of directors are tremendously powerful groups. Virtually all corporate boards and nonprofit boards have the final say on what their organizations do and how they spend money—sometimes our money. Yet boards, like all groups, are composed of individuals—people who possess skills and talents and have points of view. Who are these people, and why do they have such control?

Until the corporate scandals of the past few years, few folks outside of Wall Street even cared about corporate and nonprofit boards of directors and those who served on them. Viewed as ceremonial at best and pawns of management at worst, being on a board was more a function of who you were than what you could offer in the way of expertise. However, thanks to headline-grabbers like Enron, WorldCom, Arthur Andersen, Nortel, Tyco, and Hollinger International, there is now a new lexicon associated with boards and the responsibilities of their members. Almost everyone has heard about

Sarbanes-Oxley Legislation (US), although few could tell that it is the Accounting Reform and Investor Protection Act.

"Sarbanes-Oxley really was the catalyst for us to take a hard look at our board membership," says Greg Greenbill, president of Trident Homes. "Even though we are not publicly traded, we are responsible to our owners and want to be responsive to them as well."

According to James Waggle at the Chamber of Commerce, "Audit standards have also fueled the need to have an active, informed, and diverse group of board members. Competition for great board members is fierce. There are a handful of people out there who really understand the role of board member, and everyone would love to have them on their team. In this environment, the right board member can have an immediate impact on share prices or donations or whether the hungry get fed."

JOE VICTOR

One such "in demand" individual is Joe Victor. Joe (as he likes to be called) is the president and CEO of Allied Technology, headquartered in Chamton. Known as much for his insight into the workings of boards as for his business acumen, Joe is generally referred to as "The OnTarget Board Member" by the local business community. "Every nonprofit in town would love to have Joe Victor on their board," says Beth Blackwell, president of the Chamton Area Chamber of Commerce. "Not only does he instill confidence with donors and investors, he truly can make a difference in the future of the organization by the wisdom that he inculcates around the board table."

"I'm blessed to be able to share whatever skills I have accumulated with others," responds Joe modestly when asked. "I have had the exceeding good fortune of having others come alongside me and share, and now it's my turn."

Joe is also quick to point out that there is no magic potion. There are simply 8 behaviors that boards have to demonstrate to govern effectively."The OnTarget way really is something all boards can achieve if they simply understand their role and play it well. These are governance skills that can be taught, learned, and implemented, just as best practice management skills can be. These skills, once learned, translate to behaviors. It's these behaviors that make the difference." He even keeps a framed graphic in his office and in the Allied boardroom to remind him of these behaviors.

The 8 Indisputable Behaviors of OnTarget Board Members

1. Act on Behalf
2. Know Their Job
3. Set Targets
4. Identify Risks
5. Delegate the Work
6. Assess Performance
7. Practice Discipline
8. Report Back

THE CHAMTON FOOD BANK

One of the fortunate nonprofits is the Chamton Food Bank. Joe has served on their board for four years. "He has simply helped take us to the next level so many times," said Rebekah Monday, executive director. "Joe practices what he preaches, and it's evident in all that he does, from his own business and family to the community as a whole. A few years ago, we struggled just to keep staples on our shelves to distribute to the hungry in Chamton. Now, we operate out of numerous facilities and even help shape public policy advocating for legislative change. The credit for that rests largely with Joe and the 8 Indisputable Behaviors that he champions."

This was certainly evident on a recent Thursday night. The food bank board was meeting to look to the future. Already nationally acclaimed for their impact on hunger in Chamton, this was not a rest-on-your-laurels meeting. From the outset, it was clear that this board meant business.

The board had been communicating, over the previous six months, with the Food Bank's owners and others in Chamton about the unmet needs in the community, specifically issues and potential solutions regarding hunger and food supply.

"This is the most fundamental behavior of a good board—acting on behalf of the organization's owners," said Joe. "Even in a nonprofit, we have to make sure we're making a difference with the resources that are entrusted to us. This is accountability to the owners. It is not our money; it is others' money that we are privileged to spend in order to accomplish something, and in this case, that "something" is that no one in Chamton goes hungry."

Following the review of the information that the board had been collecting, they compared what they had heard to the existing targets, or goals, for the organization. Within an energetic and purposeful three hours, the board had modified the targets for the organization and presented it to CEO Monday for implementation. **(See Food Bank Targets—Sidebar.)**

FOOD BANK TARGETS

The Chamton Food Bank exists so that no one in Chamton goes hungry at a cost comparable to similar organizations.

- Our highest priority result will be those who are most vulnerable can deal with their own hunger.
  The most vulnerable will include new immigrants and people with disabilities.
- Public policy will value ending hunger. This result is worth at least 20 percent of resources.
- Communities will demonstrate that they value ending hunger at no more than 5 percent of organizational resources.

Clearly this board understood the essence of the business of the food bank. "None of us are experts in running a facility to alleviate hunger," says Joe. "We do, however, understand the needs in our community related to hunger sufficiently well to determine long-term organizational targets, and we empower our professional staff to achieve those targets."

Beth Blackwell at the Chamber tells it this way: "Think of it as an airplane. Our board, after talking to our members, determines the destination, how much can be spent, and even what time they would like to arrive. What they don't do is come up to the cockpit and try to fly. Instead they assess. They assess the takeoff, the ride, the landing, and even the price value equation."

"If we understand our board role well, and understand what the owners want and what the community needs from us, then we can set good targets for the organization to accomplish," says Joe. "Then we delegate achievement and come back to assess performance. It's straightforward yet requires discipline."

Nanci Oreo, the food bank's board chair, says that using the 8 Indisputable Behaviors of OnTarget Board Members has increased the satisfaction and skill levels of board members and has reduced turnover. "We tend to attract and keep the very best around our board table. We also have a highly sought-after CEO, Rebekah Monday."

NO BOARD SCHOOL

Contrast this focused behavior with the muddled and sometimes dysfunctional behavior of many boards, including school boards and city councils. According to a number of individuals, many of whom commented only on the condition of anonymity, boards can really hinder good work. "We actually dread board meetings around here," said one such person. "Staff work hard to provide good information and background, but often the board members don't even read what we give them. They either want to micromanage and criticize or are just almost completely disengaged. The energy and enthusiasm that staff could spend on providing service get sucked up dealing with the board."

"The challenge is that there is no master of board governance degree that I can send board members off to get," says Pat Cluck, executive director of the Greater United Way. "Each of our member agencies has a board, but the level of understanding of their role and value varies greatly among the boards."

Indeed, board education is an enormous dollar expense annually. If nonprofit boards and voluntary organizations in the United States and Canada combined spend as little as $1,000 each year on retreats, education, and travel, that alone would be over $2 billion. But the amount is likely much greater.

"Some of these trips are junkets, no question about it," said one board member. "Some nonprofits use the annual board trip as a means to recruit folks. Others see it as a reward for the unpaid service the board members give."

Still, most agree that the board members' motives are pure even if the execution is poor. Cluck puts it this way: "These folks generally mean well; they just don't know how they can help, because they aren't entirely clear on what they should be doing at board meetings."

THE ONTARGET BEHAVIORS

"Good governance is a differentiator," claims Joe Victor. "We don't have to be twice as good or even 25 percent better to make a huge difference. Think of a horse race or an automobile race. The horse or car that finishes first might only be a nose or a hood ahead, but it wins twice or three times as much as the other competitors. Using the 8 behaviors is not that hard and it doesn't require that much extra effort. What is it does do is give a board a competitive advantage. After all, the food bank is in competition for resources in the community. If, by using the 8 Indisputable Behaviors of OnTarget Board Members, we can be even 10 percent more efficient and effective, then the food bank can deliver dramatically better services and can make an even bigger difference in the community."

Epilogue

Six Months Later

"HELLO, IVAN. THIS IS Joe Victor."

"Well, hello, Mr. V … I mean Joe. How are you doing?"

"I'm doing great. And I'm calling because we have an opening over here at Allied for the number two spot in our PR Department. Are you ready to be OnTarget? I wonder if you want to have lunch and talk about joining our team."

Ivan smiled.

SNEAK PEEK: THE ONTARGET CEO EXECUTING THE BOARD'S PLAN

25TH ANNIVERSARY

THE BALLROOM OF THE Chamton Convention Center was decorated right up to the rafters when Joe Victor and his lovely wife Patricia entered to thunderous applause. "You know this was not my idea," Joe murmured to his wife while smiling and waving at the capacity crowd.

"I know Joe," she whispered back. "But in a sense you owe it to Allied and to the community. They have been really good to us, and this is a way to truly give back."

At this Joe gave Patricia's hand a gentle squeeze and continued to make his way through the raucous group to the head table. Although on the outside he appeared as calm and collected as he always did, mentally he was still debating with himself about his talk tonight. If he gave it as he intended the room would certainly be quieter on his exit than on his entrance. Patricia wondered at his unusual tension and decided that on this night perhaps even the unflappable Joe Victor might be nervous.

As the long-time CEO of Allied Technologies Joe had overseen a period of unprecedented growth and profitability for the company. While Joe himself was quick to give credit away, the board of Allied, along with its employees and shareholders clearly held him in high esteem and attributed much of that success to his leadership and managerial abilities. A believer in corporate and personal responsibility Joe routinely gave of his time and money to outside organizations and causes. He also balanced his home and corporate and social lives pretty well and by most every measure was successful. As a result he had been profiled in virtually every major business publication.

Lately though Joe had found himself restless. Healthy and relatively young at 59 he longed for more time to spend with his family, especially his grandchildren. The joys at work and even in the community, while real, simply did not compete with the unconstrained excitement his grandkids met him with. As soon as they became aware of his presence they stormed him with arms outstretched for hugs and pats and eye contact. “It’s a bit of a narcotic,” Joe admitted to others. “They don’t care about prestige, popularity, power or position. They just want my attention and time. With them I am just Granddad Joe.”

And so tonight Joe had every intention of deviating from the planned festivities to share an announcement that would be unexpected in most quarters.

The occasion itself was certainly significant. His 25th anniversary as CEO was quite a milestone, and his Chief of Staff, Natalie Benson and Public Information Officer Ivan John had approached him some months ago about acknowledging it in an appropriate fashion. Of course as always they knew him well, so they tied the event to a fundraiser for the Chamton United Way.

“You know, Joe,” Natalie had said in the initial conversation, “The United Way has significant capital needs. Done well this event could be good for Allied, and very good for the United Way. It would not be out of the realm of possibility that we could raise a million dollars in just this one night. That would be a great addition to their campaign.”

"And Joe," Ivan had chimed in, "We have a volunteer team here at Allied that has already agreed to handle the event. Your only requirement would be to show up and give one of your awesome speeches. And you know who would help you write that," he winked.

Even as he sat contemplating the request Joe had to admire the way they had boxed him in. "Well, I hired them," he said to himself.

"Okay," he agreed. "On one condition. Instead of a building or other edifice, any money raised would have to be used to establish a trust fund for the United Way. Only 75% of the earnings could be used annually so the fund would grow, and ideally I would like to see it go to basic services like the folks at the Food Bank or Emergency Shelter provide. We could call it The Allied Fund or something along those lines.

"Okay boss, we are on it," Natalie and Ivan beamed. "It will be the party of the year!"

As was his custom Ivan had provided a first draft of Joe's speech ninety days in advance. Ivan's relationship with Joe dated back to a feature article Ivan had done on boards of directors for the Chamton Sunday News. Everyone had referred Ivan to Joe, calling him the "OnTarget Board Member." During their interviews Joe and Ivan had hit it off, and Ivan had wound up as Assistant PIO at Allied some months later.

It had turned out to be a great partnership. Ivan truly admired Joe's leadership and as a result had helped position Joe on the national stage. As a gifted and hard working writer Ivan had become popular with the Allied team as well, and was a natural fit when the Senior PIO had retired a few years later.

With the access to Joe that Ivan enjoyed it was at times uncanny how much like Joe his first drafts sounded. This one was no exception. In fact Joe found himself admiring the tone, the timing and the message even as he reviewed it with a critical eye. The credit was given away, others were acknowledged and the Allied employees were cast in a very positive light. The challenge this time was that Joe had a different message in mind, and it was one he did not want to share even with Ivan and Natalie. Yet.

Bringing himself back to the present Joe continued to acknowledge friends and acquaintances as he and Patricia were escorted to their seats of honor at the head table. As hard as he worked at being a servant leader Joe had to admit that the applause was heady stuff. "I can see how politicians get seduced by this," he whispered to Patricia.

"Don't even go there, Joe," she whispered back. "You are gone enough now. I sure don't want you on the campaign trail!"

"Just making an observation, honey," Joe teased.

Again, though, the comment about time struck him. "Gone enough," he mused.

At that moment he made up his mind and as had so often happened to him over the years as soon as he did he immediately felt a curious sense of peace flood through him. For the first time in several days he relaxed and fully smiled.

With that sense of connection that truly close spouses enjoy Patricia sensed Joe's release of muscle tension and smiled herself. Whatever it was, Joe was happy and that made her happy too.

THE ANNOUNCEMENT

The Emcee for the evening was Nanci Oreo, the chair of the board of the Chamton Food Bank. A great speaker and leader in her own right she and Joe had worked together on the Food Bank board for many years. In that time, and with their vision and the hard work of the CEO, Rebekah Monday, the organization had grown from a fledgling food pantry to a regional force in eliminating hunger. Joe had recently chosen to rotate off of the board but stayed in touch via social media with Nanci. He was glad she was doing the event tonight because he knew she ran things with an iron hand in a velvet glove, and nothing too unusual would go on.

Even as he thought this he got his first surprise of the evening. Nanci was introducing guests, several from other Allied operations centers. Joe acknowledged each with a nod and wave. Just then Nanci said, "And of course those of us who work closely with Joe know that no celebration for him would be complete without his family. At this the side doors opened and Joe and Patricia's kids and grandkids all trooped in. The little guys were in white tuxedoes and looked darling.

Just as they reached their table in the front row the littlest one made eye contact with Joe and hollered in his outside voice, "Surprise Granddad Joe!"

The crowd roared while Joe said, "Surprise to you too River!"

After a benediction by Joe's pastor and a nice meal the festivities began in earnest. First the chair of Joe's Board spoke and told of the shareholder value increase that Allied had enjoyed during Joe's tenure. Then the Mayor herself extolled Joe's and Allied's contributions to the quality of life in Chamton. Then it was time for Allied's Chief Operating Officer, Carl Winters to announce the establishment of the Allied United Way Fund. The amount of the trust was unknown even to Joe. He had only been told that "you will be pleased" by Natalie.

As Carl explained the purpose of the trust heads nodded and people applauded. Then with a smile Carl played a DVD. The opening visual was of Joe and Pat Cluck, the CEO of the United Way. They were working on a document of some sort. They had their sleeves rolled up and were obviously engaged in the work.

"How old is that shot?" whispered Patricia.

"Boy, I don't know – several years at least," replied Joe.

Then in a great transition as the DVD wrapped up Nanci invited Joe to join her at the podium and said, "We are pleased to announce the establishment of the Allied/Victor United Way Fund. This fund will be a perpetual trust and each year three fourths of the earnings will be utilized to support basic services provided by United Way partner agencies. Tonight marks the establishment of the fund with an initial principal of," and she paused and while looking at Joe said, "3 point 75 million dollars!"

While Joe was speechless the crowd went wild. Even with Allied support this was a huge number. After a long standing ovation the crowd quieted. Each person in the audience was waiting for Joe to speak.

"Thank you Nanci!"

"Tonight is a night of celebration. And I am humbled and honored to be here among so many friends and certainly with my family."

"I will be brief tonight – I have a feeling I am going to be busy later reading bed time stories."

In unison Joe's grandsons hollered "yea!"

Again the crowd roared in delight.

Smiling Joe continued, "The years at Allied have been good ones. Patricia and I came to Chamton for a job and have stayed to make a life. We have been blessed by each of you in some way. And tonight, to have this fund established and bearing our name and the Allied name is unbelievable."

"It has long been a dream of mine."

In the back of the room Ivan and Natalie and others of Joe's inner circle at Allied smiled. This was the transition that Ivan was so good at building in for Joe.

"It has long been a dream of mine that everyone here in Chamton could enjoy the things that so many of us take for granted. A safe home. Ample food. Health and health care. An education."

"The establishment of this fund is a step in that direction and I applaud you and I thank you for your generosity."

After more applause Joe continued. "As this is a night for announcements I have one of my own."

As he paused Ivan looked at Natalie and whispered, "Whoa, that is not in the speech."

"What do you mean?" she whispered back.

Before Ivan could respond Joe continued.

"It has also long been my dream to work more directly for these things. So tonight I am sharing with you – my colleagues, my friends, and my family – that as of December 31st I will be semi-retiring from Allied. I will continue to serve on the board and act as an advisor to my successor, and I will spend at least half of my time personally volunteering on the front lines of the social services here in Chamton. I want to make a difference in the community in a personal way."

As he uttered this last phrase Joe looked directly at Patricia and winked.

At the back table Ivan and Natalie sat in stunned silence, then looked at each other and smiled and joined the applause. Allied without Joe would certainly be different, but it had been a good run. Now they could see if the succession planning they had participated in really worked.

THE BOYS AND GIRLS CLUB – SIX MONTHS LATER

Joe shook his head as he looked around the small cluttered office in the back of the Boys and Girls Club of Chamton. The facility consisted mostly of a gymnasium sized game room with pool, ping pong and foos ball tables that could be moved to allow for flexibility of use. While not necessarily run down it was long past new. The three offices at the rear of the large room looked out on the play area which was filled with children from 4 to 14. Even with the door closed the noise was pervasive. "Joe, you're not at Allied anymore!" he said to himself as he moved the blue three ring notebook over to the center of his desk and thought again of the path he had lately taken.

Following his announcement that he was going to donate a significant chunk of his time to non-profits Joe had quickly been approached by several members of the board of the Boys and Girls Club. "Joe, if you are serious about making a difference we certainly have an opportunity for you," the chair person had told him. Her name was Caroline Twist and Joe had known her for some time in her professional role as chairperson of one of the few remaining family owned local banks. In fact he considered her one of the folks in the community that really understood how to govern. Additionally

Patricia was active with her in the Women's Service League of Chamton and spoke glowingly of her leadership there.

Caroline continued, "As you know Joe the youth of today are the leaders of tomorrow, and no one has a better track record than the Boys and Girls Clubs. We have an incredible list of success stories. Folks like Denzel Washington, General Wesley Clark, Shaquille O'Neal and many others. Our programs work, but our burnout at the Executive Director level is incredible. We simply struggle at that position. The people that are most successful in the club environment love kids and are fine in their sphere. When it comes to managing the finances, the fundraising and the functions of the executive suite they crash and burn. Consequently boards struggle, the staff struggles and we do not impact as many kids as we otherwise could. In fact we have a vacancy at the top now and no internal candidates we are comfortable with."

"Well," said Joe, "You have articulated the issue, and I can certainly sympathize. What does that have to do with me?"

"Well, echoed Caroline, looking around at her fellow board members for support, "Joe, we want you to take on an interim role as CEO of the Chamton Club."

As Joe started to shake his head Caroline held up her hand. "Now Joe, before you answer let me amplify a bit. The Board uses a similar governance model to Allied. In fact you will certainly recall that you helped us with that a few years ago."

Joe nodded, seeing now where this was going. He began to smile.

Caroline took this as a good sign and continued. "We have been in contact with the folks at National and they have given us the green light to use you as a pilot project. If you can take the governance model and fully implement it in the organization here in Chamton National has agreed to replicate it in all of the large clubs. You could impact hundreds – even thousands – of young people. Come on Joe, you said yourself you want to make a difference. What better place? What better time? Who better than the OnTarget Board Member?"

Does Joe take the interim role??
Can good governance be implemented at the staff level??
What would an OnTarget staff look like??
Look for the *OnTarget CEO: Executing the Board's Plan* – to be released in 2013!

APPENDICES

- Appendix 1—The 8 Indisputable Behaviors of OnTarget Board Members
- Appendix 2—Allied Technologies, Board Policy Index, Staff Boundaries
- Appendix 3—Chamton Food Bank, Board Agenda
- Appendix 4—Chamton Food Bank Board Policy, "Board Authority: Governing Style"
- Appendix 5—Chamton Food Bank Board Policy, "Staff Boundaries: Treatment of Clients"
- Appendix 6—Chamton Food Bank, CEO Report on Compliance with Board Policy on Staff Boundaries: Treatment of Clients
- Appendix 7—Chamton Food Bank Board Policy, "Board Targets"
- Appendix 8—Chamton Food Bank, CEO Report on Achievement of Board Targets

Appendix I

The 8 Indisputable Behaviors of OnTarget Board Members

ONTARGET BOARD MEMBERS DO the following:

1. **Act on behalf** of their owners—they identify their owners, seek their views and values, and use them in decision making.
2. **Know their job**, the business of the organization, and their duties under law, and they continually educate and orient themselves.
3. **Set targets** for the organization—they determine certain outcomes for certain beneficiaries at a certain cost based on owners' wants and on knowledge of the internal and external business environments and then the board writes them down for staff.
4. **Identify the risks** in the organization that are unacceptable and write them down as boundaries on staff actions.
5. **Delegate the work** by setting targets and boundaries, giving them to the staff and letting them do the work.
6. **Assess performance** by checking to see if the organization has hit the target and avoided the risks.

7. **Practice discipline** in orientation, meeting attendance, preparedness, participation, discussion, focus, and the avoidance of conflicts of interest.
8. **Report back** to the owners on the progress toward "hitting the target."

Appendix 2

Allied Technologies Board Policy Index Staff Boundaries

GENERAL STAFF BOUNDARIES

THE CEO MAY NOT cause or allow any condition, decision, activity, or organizational circumstance that is unlawful, imprudent, or unethical.

1. Treatment of Customers
   With respect to interactions with customers, the CEO may not cause or allow conditions, procedures, decisions, or activities that are unsafe, disrespectful, untimely, or unnecessarily intrusive.
2. Treatment of Staff
   With respect to treatment of staff, the CEO may not cause or allow conditions that are unfair, disorganized, undignified, or unclear.
3. Financial Planning
   The CEO shall not cause or allow financial planning for any fiscal year or the remaining part of any fiscal year to deviate materially from the board's target priorities, risk financial jeopardy, or fail to be derived from a multiyear plan.
4. Financial Condition
   With respect to the actual, ongoing financial condition and activities, the CEO shall not cause or allow

the development of financial jeopardy or material deviation of actual expenditures from board priorities established in target policies.

5. Protection of Assets
   The CEO shall not cause or allow corporate assets to be unprotected, inadequately maintained, or unnecessarily risked.
6. Compensation and Benefits
   With respect to employment, compensation, and benefits to employees and contract workers, the CEO shall not cause or allow jeopardy to financial integrity or public image.
7. Communication to the Board
   The CEO shall not cause or allow the board to be uninformed or unsupported in its work.

Adapted from *Reinventing Your Board: A Step-by-Step Guide to Implementing Policy Governance*

Appendix 3

Chamton Food Bank
Board Agenda
Allied Technologies Boardroom
December 3, 2011

Start Time	Time Allo-cated	Item	Outcome	Reference Docu-mentation
5:00 PM	10 minutes	Gathering	Group check-in and introductions Board adoption of meeting agenda	Document #1 in board package
5:10	10 minutes	Meeting roles	Appointment of meeting monitor	
5:20	5 minutes	Approval of minutes	Board motion for approval	Document #2 in board package
5:25	5 minutes	Required approvals	Decision on approval required	Document #3—"Request for Funding to the Chamton Community Foundation" and attached CEO compliance report
5:30	20 minutes	Assessment of compliance treatment of clients	Decision on assess-ment of compliance report: Reasonable interpre-tation? Proof of compliance?	As circulated November 15, 2011, by e-mail from CEO
5:50	2 hours	Target policies	Decision on amend-ments to board policies	Document #4 in board package
7:50	10 minutes	Meeting monitor report	Information for board self-assessment	
8:00		Adjournment		

Appendix 4

Chamton Food Bank Board Policy

Category: Board Authority	*Title: Governing Style*
Policy No: 3-2	*Date of Adoption: April 2008* *Date of Revision: August 2010*

THE BOARD WILL GOVERN with an emphasis on (1) outward vision rather than an internal preoccupation, (2) encouragement of diversity in viewpoints, (3) strategic leadership more than administrative detail, (4) clear distinction of board and chief executive roles, (5) collective rather than individual decisions, (6) future rather than past or present, and (7) proactivity rather than reactivity.

Accordingly,

1. The board will cultivate a sense of group responsibility. The board, not the staff, will be responsible for excellence in governing. The board will be an initiator of policy, not merely a reactor to staff initiatives. The board will use the expertise of individual members to enhance the ability of the board as a body, rather than to substitute the individual for the board's values.
2. The board will direct, control, and inspire the organization through the careful establishment of broad written policies reflecting the board's values and perspectives about ends to be achieved and means to

be avoided. The board's major policy focus will be on the intended long-term impacts outside the operating organization.

3. The board will enforce upon itself whatever discipline is needed to govern with excellence. Discipline will apply to matters such as attendance, preparation, policy-making principles, respect of roles, and ensuring the continuity of governance capability.
4. Continual board development will include orientation of new members in the board's governance process and periodic board discussion of process improvement.
5. The board will monitor and discuss the board's process and performance at each meeting. Self-monitoring will include comparison of board activity and discipline to policies in the Board Authority and Delegation to the CEO categories.

Adapted from *Boards that Make a Difference: A New Design for Leadership in Nonprofit and Public Organizations*.

Appendix 5

Chamton Food Bank Board Policy

Category: Staff Boundaries	*Title: Treatment of Clients*
Policy No: 2	*Date of Adoption: April 2008* *Date of Revision: August 2011*

WITH RESPECT TO INTERACTIONS with clients, the CEO will not cause or allow conditions that are undignified, unsafe, or unnecessarily intrusive.

Appendix 6

Chamton Food Bank CEO Report on Compliance with Board Policy on Staff Boundaries: Treatment of Clients November 2011

THIS IS MY REPORT on compliance with the board policy on Treatment of Clients 2-2.

I certify that the following is true.

Signed Rebekah Monday

POLICY

With respect to interactions with clients, the CEO will not cause or allow conditions that are undignified, unsafe, or unnecessarily intrusive.

CEO INTERPRETATION:

I interpret "undignified" to mean that after delivering a questionnaire to a random sample of clients ($N = 1{,}500$), we will find that 90 percent of respondents agree that staff and volunteers took time to understand their needs and 90 percent of respondents agree they were not laughed at or made fun of by staff or volunteers and were not served by staff or volunteers using voice tones that were patronizing.

Rationale: The National Psychological Association states that if people are treated in patronizing ways and feel their needs are not understood, they will feel a lack of dignity. The National Association of Food Bank Networks reports that clients of food banks, already feeling badly about having to use this service, will feel a further loss of dignity if they feel they are not understood or are patronized. The 90 percent goal is reasonable in both instances, as the National Psychological Association reports that there will always be at least 10 percent of respondents who will report dissatisfaction with the way they were served by service staff, because their overall experience is influenced by other external factors. I used a reliable and valid survey as determined by the local university's marketing research department.

Data:

92 percent agreed staff and volunteers took time to understand their needs.

93 percent agreed they were not laughed at or made fun of by staff or volunteers and were not served by staff or volunteers using voice tones that were patronizing.

I therefore report compliance.

CEO INTERPRETATION:

I interpret "unsafe" to mean that food is handled and prepared in the food kitchens under conditions that are compliant with industry standards 100 percent of the time, as found by an inspection by USDA inspectors.

Rationale: The USDA states that preparing and handling food in unsafe ways can cause foodborne illness, which would be unsafe to clients. The 100 percent goal is reasonable according to the National Association of Food Networks, who state that food prepared and handled in amounts to be served to such large numbers must be of the highest level of safety due to the great risk of contamination leading to illness.

Data: 92 percent compliance in the latest inspection by USDA inspectors in January 2012.

I report non-compliance and attached is my plan to bring operations into compliance.

CEO INTERPRETATION:

I interpret "unnecessarily intrusive" to mean that a National Privacy Commission audit will find 100 percent of the time that information routinely collected from clients is used only in the assessment and provision of services to those clients.

Rationale: The National Privacy Commission (NPC) states in their Privacy Regulations for Community Service Organizations that information, unless the client is otherwise explicitly informed, is to be collected from the client only in order to provide direct service. One hundred percent compliance with these regulations is expected by this agency.

Data: The NPC audit conducted in September 2011 showed 100 percent compliance.

I report compliance..

Appendix 7

Chamton Food Bank Board Policy

Category: Board Targets	*Title:*
Policy No: 1-1	*Date of Adoption: April 2008* *Date of Revision: April 2010*

THE CHAMTON FOOD BANK *exists so that no one in Chamton goes hungry at a cost comparable to similar organizations.*

1. Our highest-priority result will be that those who are most vulnerable can deal with their own hunger.
2. Public policy will value ending hunger: this result is worth at least 20 percent of resources.
3. Communities will demonstrate that they value ending hunger at no more than 5 percent of organizational resources.

Appendix 8

Chamton Food Bank CEO Report on Achievement of Board Targets June 2012

BOARD POLICY

THE CHAMTON FOOD BANK *exists so that no one in Chamton goes hungry at a cost comparable to other similar organizations.*

1. Our highest-priority result will be that those who are most vulnerable can deal with their own hunger.
2. Public policy will value ending hunger: this result is worth at least 20 percent of resources.
3. Communities will demonstrate that they value ending hunger at no more than 5 percent of organizational resources.

CEO REPORT

With the exception of the phrase "a cost justified by the results," I believe that the board has comprehensively interpreted this policy in its subsequent policy provisions. My interpretations and data are attached to those provisions.

Board Policy Wording	CEO's Interpretation	Rationale	Data/Proof
The Chamton food bank exists so that no one in Chamton goes hungry at a cost comparable to other similar organizations	Persons will have adequate nourishment for no more than \$18 per person.	The UN Study on Hunger has determined that the only useful definition of "not going hungry" is adequate nourishment inasmuch as hunger can be diminished by non-nourishing foodstuffs. The National Institute of Performance and Productivity has identified two comparator organizations, the Harvest Food Bank of Greater Mytown and the Food Bank of Metroplace, as top award winners in organizations in producing maximum benefit for the cost. These two organizations, with similar population size, demographics, and results, are considered now to be operating at maximum productivity and efficiency, producing similar results at a cost of \$17.50 per person served.	Our cost this year is \$17.97 per person. I report compliance.
1. Our highest-priority result will be that those who are most vulnerable can deal with their own hunger.	1.A. 10 percent of people in Chamton living below 150 percent of the poverty level will get at least one meal every day.	The Census Bureau data show that people living in Chamton need at least 150 percent of the poverty level to meet basic needs. The Census Bureau and the UN Study on Hunger agree that people below that level are most vulnerable to not having enough food to eat because of lack of money.	Our 2010 hunger study—"Who Is Hungry in Chamton?"—provides the following data: People living below 150 percent poverty level = 130,000 10 percent of this population = 13,000 13,000 × 1 meal per day × 365 days = 4,745,000

Board Policy Wording	CEO's Interpretation	Rationale	Data/Proof
		The UN Study on Hunger reports that people living below the poverty level access food through various other resources: Own/family resources = 50 percent Food stamps = 18 percent Free school lunch = 6 percent Other agencies = 16 percent This leaves approximately 10 percent of the population without a reliable source for food.	Last year we served 4.8 million meals. I report compliance.
	1.B. I also interpret this policy to mean that 40 percent of food bank clients surveyed will report that they: • have access on a weekly basis to nonperishable food items, fresh produce, and bread items to feed themselves and their family for a week; • know how to plan meals that are nutritious and economical; and • know where to buy and how to prepare food that is nutritious and economical.	The Government Office of Nutrition Policy and Promotion research shows that people who are given the skills and knowledge to plan meals and buy and prepare food can deal with their own hunger most effectively. The research shows that they eat more nutritiously for the same or less money. The National Association on Hunger reports that on average less than 50 percent of the clients of a food bank will have the time to learn skills and gain knowledge. They agree that 40 percent is a reasonable target.	Our 2010 hunger study—"Who Is Hungry in Chamton?"—which surveyed 5,000 clients, shows that 41 percent of our clients have access on a weekly basis to nonperishable food items, fresh produce, and bread items to feed themselves and their family for a week. The same report shows that 38 percent of our clients report that they have the skills and knowledge to plan meals and buy and prepare food. I report compliance.

Board Policy Wording	CEO's Interpretation	Rationale	Data/Proof
	1.C. I also interpret this policy to mean that 100 percent of school-age children in Chamton will begin their school day with breakfast.	The National Report on Child Poverty says that children have the lowest capacity to earn money and thus control their own food intake. The latest research reported by the Department of Education, in "Learning: What We Eat Makes a Difference," says that children who, on a regular basis, do not eat breakfast have learning difficulties, specifically resulting in lower scores in math and reading. It also says that proper nutrition is vital to the growth and development of children. In the long term, improved learning will result in their being able to attain better employment and thereby break the hunger and poverty cycle. According to the 2011 Census, of those living below the 150 percent poverty line, 59 percent are children. The most readily reachable group of children is made up of those in the school system. The Chamton School District 2011 classroom survey reports that 23.2 percent of children come to school hungry each day.	The Chamton School District 2011 classroom survey shows that no children started the school day hungry. I report compliance.

Board Policy Wording	CEO's Interpretation	Rationale	Data/Proof
	I interpret "highest priority" for this entire policy to mean that at least 70 percent of resources will be allocated to the achievement of this target.		Attached is this year's budget showing the allocations per target policy. 75 percent of resources are allocated to this target policy. I therefore report compliance.
2. Public policy will value ending hunger: this result is worth at least 20 percent of resources.	2.A.I interpret this to mean that 75% of municipal Councilors will report that they understand the main issues and perspectives regarding the need for increasing municipally funded housing stock targeted at low-income people.	This is a complex topic with a diverse number of citizen perspectives and often the loudest voices get heard. Policy decision making is influenced by many factors. People who use the food bank often have no voice, and so this organization is best positioned to be able to influence policy makers.	The annual survey completed by the Citizens for Responsive Governance reported that 9 of our 10 Councilors understood the issues. I report compliance.
3. Communities will demonstrate that they value ending hunger at no more than 5 percent of organizational resources.	3.A. In our community, volunteerism for hunger-related causes will increase over previous years.	People demonstrate their belief in interdependence and in giving and sharing by donating their time and money to nonprofit organizations. This is well documented, most recently in the research paper "Volunteerism in North America: Its History and Future." The paper also states that citizens will demonstrate, by volunteering, their level of interest in or value to a cause, in this case, in ending hunger. An increase in the number of people who volunteer in food banks, churches, and food drives would be a tangible demonstration of this.	Charity at Home reports an increase in the rate of volunteerism to hunger-related causes of 1.6 percent over the previous year in the municipality of Chamton. I report compliance.

Board Policy Wording	CEO's Interpretation	Rationale	Data/Proof
	3.B. Donations of money and food from community members, including community service organizations, churches, schools, grocery stores, food processors, and farmers, will be maintained at least at current levels.	Charity at Home, America's number one independent charity evaluator, reports that due to an increase in the last three years worldwide in natural disasters, donations locally have been declining. This organization advises that nonprofit organizations that maintain their current level of donations are considered successful.	Charity at Home reports an increase in donations to food causes of 1 percent over last year. I report compliance.

Authors' Biographies

MICHAEL A. (MIKE) CONDUFF

MICHAEL A. (MIKE) CONDUFF is the President and CEO of The Elim Group - *Your Governance Experts*, a governance, leadership, speaking and consulting firm. Mike has 35+ years of leadership, management and governance experience, having served as the City Manager of four highly acclaimed University communities in the United States.

Mike earned his B.S. in civil engineering at the University of New Hampshire, graduating Cum Laude. His M.B.A. is from Pittsburg State University. He is also a charter graduate of the Carver Policy Governance® Academy and is a Past Chair of the Board of Directors of the International Policy Governance® Association. Mike has a number of national and international not-for-profit, for-profit and local government clients. His success in dealing with Boards has earned him the reputation of being the "Go-To Guy" for council retreats and corporate governance.

In addition Mike is a bestselling author, and has written or co-authored numerous books, including *Pushing to the Front,* with Brian Tracy, *The Success Secret,* with Jack Canfield, *Democracy at the Doorstep – True Stories from the Green Berets of Public Administrators, Bottom Line Green – How America's Cities are Saving the Planet (And Money Too!)* with Jim Hunt, *The OnTarget Board Member – 8 Indisputable Behaviors,* and

The Policy Governance® Fieldbook, a book on the practical applications of Policy Governance. He writes a regular column in the internationally distributed *Public Manager* magazine, and is a contributing author for the internationally acclaimed "Green Book" series for ICMA.

As a much sought after and frequent keynote speaker at national and international events, Mike regularly receives "best of the conference" accolades from attendees and conference planners.

Mike is a Fellow in the prestigious National Academy of Public Administration. He has been honored with the 2006 TCMA Mentoring Award in memory of Gary Gwyn, the 2004 International Award for Career Development in Memory of L. P. (Perry) Cookingham from ICMA, and the especially meaningful Joy Sansom Mentor Award from the Urban Management Assistants of North Texas for his commitment to helping others achieve their potential. The Center for Digital Government awarded Mike their coveted "Best of Texas Visionary Award."

Mike's traces his Native American roots to his Great Grandfather, and attributes his love of motivational speaking and telling stories to his grandmothers. He is a Past President of both the Texas City Management Association and Kansas City Management Association. He was one of the original cohort of fully credentialed members of the International City/County Management Association, and is a past member of its Executive Board, where he chaired the Finance Committee. He still serves ICMA as their Senior Advisor for Governance.

www.TheElimGroup.com

CAROL M. GABANNA

Carol Gabanna's passion is learning – her client's, her colleague's and her own. She counts herself as one of those who loves her work and gets to do work that draws on her talents. Carol's talents are in stimulating personal and group excellence, whether it is coaching an executive, teaching a group of managers how to manage employee performance, facilitating an organization's strategic planning or teaching a board how to govern their non profit organization. Carol draws on her experiences in a variety of large and small organizations as a manager, a CEO, a board member and an employee. Carol is a consultant with HRA, a human resource consulting firm in Atlantic Canada delivering customized training and facilitation solutions to public sector, private sector and non profit clients.

Carol received her BBA at the University of Prince Edward Island. She was a manager in a hospital, then CEO of a non profit health organization. Carol worked for 5 years for the Province of PEI as a member of a team of internal consultants, delivering training and facilitation to managers and employees in the public sector. Carol most recently was with a community college delivering contract training and facilitation in the areas of personal and organizational development. Carol is a certified Executive Coach and has a Graduate Certificate in Executive Coaching from Royal Roads University.

Carol is co-author of *The Policy Governance Fieldbook: Practical Lessons, Tips and Tools from the Experiences of Real –World Boards*. She has published numerous articles in several national publications. Carol is a past board member of the International Policy Governance Association and has consulted with boards of organization large and small in many fields including: health, education, arts, heritage, family violence, literacy, and workers compensation. Carol regularly serves as a volunteer consultant and coach to boards in her home town.

While she loves all the training and facilitation that she does, governance training and consulting is her passion. She says, “The job of the board is critical, the board members’ time is precious. There is wisdom in ordinary people and what fuels my passion is finding ways to draw out and connect with that wisdom, especially in all of those ordinary, but special people who sit on boards.”

www.CarolGabanna.com

CATHERINE M. RASO

Catherine M. Raso BA MBA is President of CMR Governance Consulting, a governance consulting firm. Founded in 1996, and located in Hamilton, Ontario, just outside of Toronto, Canada, CMR Governance Consulting helps public, non-profit, private and governmental boards of directors to improve their governance systems, structures and processes.

A highly skilled and experienced facilitator, trainer and coach, Catherine has earned a reputation for listening to her clients' special circumstances, and responding with options for solutions that make sense based on an individual board's goals. She has consulted with more than 300 boards around the world and has an impressive client list.

Catherine earned her BA (Economics) and MBA (Health Services Management) from McMaster University. She is fully trained and highly experienced in the theory and implementation of the Policy Governance® model (Academy graduate, Atlanta, 1995)

Catherine was CEO, for 12 years, of a non-profit retail organization in the health care industry and has served on many local community boards, including arts, service and educational organizations.

Catherine is co-author of *The Policy Governance Fieldbook: Practical Lessons, Tips and Tools from the Experience of Real-World Boards* (Jossey-Bass, 1999) and author of the soon to be released governance book, *100 Ways to Build a Better Board* (NVP Publishing, 2012).

Catherine has more than 25 years experience as a volunteer governance trainer and workshop facilitator with local United Ways, and has instructed in non-profit management courses at the college and university levels. Catherine's contribution to her community includes working as a volunteer governance coach with local small non-profit boards each year.

Catherine lives in Hamilton, Ontario with her husband Joe, and their 3 children (now young adults), Natalie, Victor and Patricia.

Catherine's excitement about good governance and her professional commitment is summed up in a quote by Katharine Graham, *"To love what you do, and feel that it matters—how could anything be more fun?"*

www.CatherineRaso.com

Bibliography

Carver, J. *Boards That Make a Difference: A New Design for Leadership in Nonprofit and Public Organizations*, 3rd ed. San Francisco, Jossey-Bass, 2006.

Carver, J. and Carver, M. (eds.). *Board Leadership: Policy Governance in Action (*Successor to *Board Leadership: A Bimonthly Workshop with John Carver,* 1992- 1998). Bimonthly. San Francisco: Jossey-Bass, 1998-2006.

Carver, J . and Carver, M. *Reinventing Your Board: A Step-by-Step Guide to Implementing Policy Governance, Revised ed.* San Francisco, Jossey-Bass, 2006.

Collins, J. *Good to Great: Why Some Companies Make the Leap...and Others Don't,* New York, Harper Collins Canada, 2001.

Greenleaf, R. *The Servant as Leader.* Indianapolis: The Greenleaf Center, 1982.

Greenleaf, R. *Trustee as Servant.* Indianapolis: The Greenleaf Center, 1974.

Oliver, C. (gen. ed.), with Conduff, M., Edsall, S., Gabanna, C., Loucks, R., Paszkiewicz, D., Raso, C., and Stier, L. *The Policy Governance Fieldbook: Practical Lessons, Tips, and Tools from the Experiences of Real-World Boards.* San Francisco: Jossey-Bass, 1999.